9 Ar [illegible]

Fadlan –

Africa

is sometimes

a lonely sea –

But

All my

[illegible]

DECLARING
INDEPENDENCE

DECLARING ✦✦✦
INDEPENDENCE

✦✦✦✦✦✦✦ The Beginning of the End
of the Two-Party System

Douglas E. Schoen

RANDOM HOUSE / NEW YORK

Published in the United States by Random House, an imprint of The Random House Publishing Group, a division of Random House, Inc., New York.

Library of Congress Cataloging-in-Publication Data

Schoen, Douglas E.
Declaring independence : the beginning of the end of the two-party system /
Douglas E. Schoen.
p. cm.
ISBN 978-1-4000-6733-6
1. Party affiliation—United States. 2. Third parties (United States politics)
3. United States—Politics and government—2001– I. Title.
JK2271.S35 2008
324.273—dc22   2007040001

Printed in the United States of America on acid-free paper

www.atrandom.com

1 2 3 4 5 6 7 8 9

First Edition

Book design by Susan Turner

To my parents

Contents

Preface

MY REASONS FOR WRITING THIS BOOK ARE FAIRLY STRAIGHTFORWARD.
I believe that we are facing a crisis in America, and that the crisis
goes well beyond simple concerns about the way our political system operates.

To be sure, there are high levels of cynicism in America. There
is a sense that our country has been too polarized and divided, as
well as a clear perception that the political system is not doing a
good job resolving our problems. But, as I argue in the book, our
problems run much deeper than that. We simply are facing
crises—with the war in Iraq, the war on terror, immigration, re-
forming entitlements and health care, for example—that appear
to go beyond the ability of the two parties to successfully resolve
outstanding differences by developing commonsense solutions.
These are literally life-and-death questions for our nation. They

go to the heart of who we are as a people. And it has been my view that both parties have demonstrated a singular inability to deal with those problems in a practical, collegial, results-oriented fashion.

It is my contention that third-party candidates in America have frequently been better able to influence the political process in a constructive way than the two parties themselves alone. Consequently, I believe that a third-party candidate running on a platform of coherent compromise, tough-minded conciliation, and candid, clear-eyed bipartisanship can achieve much to help resolve the seemingly intractable differences that exist between the two parties.

I have been a political consultant and analyst for more than thirty years. I am proud of what I have done, and I am proud of the people I have worked for, who have been mostly, but not exclusively, Democrats. Some of my best political and personal experiences have come during my work for Bill and Hillary Clinton, whom I have happily supported and worked for in past campaigns. I also could not be more supportive of the work of Mayor Mike Bloomberg in New York City, another former client, who has put into action many of the principles outlined in the book.

This work has been written not to advocate for any individual candidate, nor has it been written to criticize or blame specific politicians or political parties. There is enough blame to go around, and at this point, I think it is less a question of pointing a finger at individuals or parties than of trying to recommend ways to fix a system that has become dysfunctional and seemingly closed to new ideas and new approaches.

I write this as a clarion call to America that we need to come together and cast aside ideologically driven, partisan considerations. Hopefully a third-party candidate will emerge who can raise the questions and issues outlined below in a serious and sustained way. But even if that does not happen, my hope is that this book will impel the leadership of the two parties and their respective presidential candidates to recognize that the American people are angry and that they are demanding that their political leaders come together to address pragmatically the very difficult problems facing America.

And make no mistake about it. If this does not happen, and we face another four years of political paralysis, the net losers will clearly be the American people.

Introduction

Right now, both parties are way too far apart and nobody is looking out for the good of the people.

—GARY BUTLER, 60, Show Low, Arizona

The independent vote is swinging everything. They're going to be the powerhouse.

—HAL F. BUTLER, 81, Gary Butler's father

THOSE FATHER-AND-SON COMMENTS SUM UP THE STATE OF AMERICA. A massive shift in the landscape of the nation's politics has occurred; typical voters, the sensible, honest, hardworking folks from the heartland, disgruntled Republicans and Democrats alike, are abandoning the status quo and looking for alternatives. They've heard enough from the candidates of the two major political parties. Congressional gridlock has become an inside-the-Beltway cliché. They've had it with the carefully scripted, lip-service rhetoric, the vetted speeches that pander to special-interest groups, and the business-as-usual governance that reveals a nation that too often is running in place. They see political parties that have been captured by their respective left and right wings, which don't speak to the average concerns and fears of the electorate at large. Our political leaders are no longer fooling most of the people most of the time. The electorate has spoken (check the results of the 2006 midterm election) and they want change—fundamental change. And that change goes beyond replacing Republicans with Democrats and vice versa.

We're entering a new world of politics, a realm that reflects the prevailing mood of the nation, but its meaning goes much deeper than simple disaffection with the status quo. The American people are tired of the bickering among their political leaders, and they're starved for something new. It's not about left or right, or liberals or neocons or other subidentities within the prevailing two-party system. And it's not just about a shift toward discovering a sensible moderate who can pull us together, although that is certainly part of it. We've undergone a secular change in politics, and you can see it in living rooms everywhere across the nation. People are no longer drinking the Kool-Aid from the Sunday morning talking heads; they're looking past ideologues for a rational problem solver with an achievable agenda.

As *New York Times* columnist David Brooks recently put it, "Today, post-9/11, most Americans aren't anxious because their freedoms are being impinged. They're anxious because there's chaos all around: foreign policy chaos, fiscal chaos, cultural chaos. The authority structures they rely on have let them down."

After he taught a course in political theory at Duke University, Brooks noted how young voters are taking the lead in this thinking. He wrote, "I'm struck by the universal tone of post-boomer pragmatism. . . . If my Duke students are representative, then the U.S. is about to see a generation that is practical, anti-ideological, modest and centrist (maybe to a fault)."

I've seen firsthand this shift that Brooks has noted, and it's just as widespread as he surmises, and goes well beyond the nation's youth. There is a broad, sweeping movement in America that is rapidly buying into the notion that we're entering a new era when pandering sound bites just won't cut it anymore. Brooks also noted that Mike Huckabee and Barack Obama had seen their ratings improve because they both represent the kind of consensus-driven politics that emphasizes unity and concili-ation rather than ideological purity. Frank Rich of *The New York Times* has reached the same conclusion: "Though their views on issues are often antithetical, Mr. Huckabee and Mr. Obama may be united in catching the wave of an emerging zeitgeist that is larger than either party's ideology. An exhausted and disillu-sioned public may be ready for" more conciliatory messages that emphasize unity and compassion.

As Chuck Todd, the political director of NBC News, put it after the November 2007 state and local elections, "Just how angry is the electorate? Perhaps angrier than any of us imagined. It's not just anger, however, that voters are expressing toward politicians. It appears to be downright distrust with the govern-ment itself." The result, Todd concluded, was an electorate seek-ing "unconventional change." That change, in my view, could take the form of a fundamental alteration in the makeup and look of our political parties. According to a poll taken by the firm I founded, Penn, Schoen & Berland, 61 percent of voters say the two major parties are failing and that having an independent on the ballot in the 2008 presidential election would be good for America.

Three out of five Americans. More than the plurality and major-ity that elected Bush in 2000 and 2004.

Independent voters now make up the largest segment of the Ameri-can electorate. Evidence that voters are generally unhappy with today's Democratic and Republican parties is mounting every-where. According to the American National Election Studies at the University of Michigan and Stanford University, indepen-dents made up 38 percent of the electorate in 2004 and 33 percent of those who actually voted. In swing states like Florida, the number of unaffiliated voters has more than tripled, climbing from 527,000 in 1994 to almost 1.9 million today, while in Pennsylvania and North Carolina, the number has increased threefold, totaling more than one million today in each state. In New Jersey, unaffiliated voters now make up 58.7 percent of the electorate.

Polls taken by such news organizations as Fox News, NBC, and *The Wall Street Journal,* as well as by think tanks such as the Pew Research Center, have consistently found that at least 50 percent of Americans want to see a third-party candidate on their ballots. Blue state or red state, half the nation is in a downright disagreeable mood. The Luntz, Maslansky group, a Republican polling firm, found that 81 percent of the electorate said they would consider voting for a qualified independent presidential candidate in 2008. And polling done in September and October 2007 by Scott Rasmussen showed Colin Powell in a statistical tie with Barack Obama and Rudy Giuliani in a trial heat, and in second place, nine points behind Hillary Clinton and ahead of Rudy Giuliani in an additional ballot test.

Other data, while not quite as substantial as Luntz's and Rasmussen's, points to the same conclusion. A *Washington Post*/Kaiser Family Foundation/Harvard University survey of candidates in May–June 2007 found that 58 percent of the electorate said they would seriously consider voting for an independent in 2008. Over three-quarters of independents gave this response, as did about half of Democrats and Republicans. *USA Today*/Gallup data collected at about the same time (July 2007) confirms this basic view. They found that the percentage saying a third party was needed because the major parties do such a poor job had gone from 40 percent in late 2003, to 48 percent in the fall of 2006, to 58 percent in July 2007. Only one-third of those surveyed in July 2007 said the major parties do an adequate job representing the American people.

While the actual results of individual surveys may differ, the conclusion is clear. A solid majority of the American people will actively consider voting for a third-party candidate in 2008. This means that somewhere between *72 million* and *96 million* voters (based on the 2004 turnout—you can bet it will be at least as large in 2008) are searching, forever hopeful, for some reasonable alternative, a leader who is not a traditional Republican or Democrat.

There is no dispute that American politics is dangerously mired in a dysfunctional two-party system. Theodore J. Lowi, a prominent Cornell University professor, wrote, "Two-party competition has turned from a public good to a public evil. The two-party system has at the moment become a menace to the Republic, made worse by the overwhelming weakness of the parties' presidential candidates and the impossibility of choosing between them when the only way to vote no for the candidate you hate is to vote yes for the one you can barely tolerate. And forget about having a good option when you hate both equally." Similarly, former House Speaker Newt Gingrich, once a devout partisan, has recently concluded that the 2008 candidates are failing both parties and the voters. Echoing Lowi, a man of the left, Gingrich has concluded that the real divisions are not between Democrats and Republicans or red states and blue states. Rather, "the real division is between hard-working tax-paying Americans—of both parties and all races—and an entrenched permanent governing system in Washington and state capitals designed to serve its own needs and not the needs of the people."

Not surprisingly, Americans feel alienated from the two major parties, with one poll showing 47 percent of voters saying that Democrats don't share their values and 53 percent saying the same of Republicans. Two out of five Americans cannot name *anything they like* about the Democratic Party, and nearly half of those polled cannot name *anything they like* about the Republicans. Two-thirds of the voters say the two political parties need to be held accountable. Almost half of all American voters say the country is better off when no single party controls both the White House and the Congress, and they also believe in the notion of an independent political candidate.

What, then, is the alternative?

The situation is ripe, I believe, for a third-party candidate as part of the fundamental change I've spoken of above.

We're facing huge challenges—for example, how do we satisfy our long-term energy needs, at reasonable prices, while decreasing our dependence on oil and the governments that export it? That's just one big question. Unfortunately, neither Republicans nor Democrats have offered comprehensive solutions, because they may require sacrifice today for gain tomorrow; the short-term fix is try to please everyone whose hand you shake so you can earn his vote in the next election. We need some sage, creative, long-term solutions to intractable problems.

We also need a third-party candidate to confront issues and policy options the two major parties have been loath to confront. Democrats, for example, have been extremely reluctant to advocate cutting entitlement programs. Republicans are similarly afraid to advocate tax increases. It will take an independent candidate to consider these options separately or, more likely, together.

The candidates think about "issues"; the voters worry about their problems. Politicians have an agenda that seeks to offend the fewest people possible, especially the activists in their own party, especially during primary season; the voters have a misery index that has nothing to do with partisan political considerations. And right now they feel miserable. The coming campaign will be fought over the critical items: a balanced budget, the trade deficit, energy independence, the war in Iraq and terrorism, entitlement reform, immigration, and health care. We need to fashion long-term solutions to these problems sooner rather than later.

We're burdened by dispatching troops to Afghanistan and Iraq, and now there is saber rattling about Iran and the possibility of

other conflicts breaking out in the Middle East. We're a net importing nation, not an exporting one, and it hurts our economy.
(China has become a major creditor, and it's a good thing we're
their biggest customer; otherwise, they would have called in their
notes long ago.) The first batch of 77 million baby boomers will be
quitting work soon, and there won't be enough money in the Social
Security and Medicare coffers to carry them through their retirement years, as Robert Samuelson recently noted in a *Newsweek*
column. Samuelson was advocating a broad-based, nonpartisan,
think-tank-driven process to force politicians of both parties to
address the problem of an aging population seriously.

This dovetails with another issue. We're living longer. We're
taking care of our elderly parents. Someone has to pay for all the
pills and new diagnostic and treatment technologies. Health-care
costs have spiraled upward dramatically, taxing our Medicare and
Medicaid programs. Nearly fourteen years ago, President Clinton
warned Congress that a national health crisis was looming;
37 million Americans were uninsured. The crisis is now here:
nearly 46 million Americans went without health insurance in
2005. We all have to shoulder the costs incurred by those without
health coverage.

Where's the plan or even the principles Democrats and Republicans can agree on? They don't exist.

We need a sound national energy policy, and right now the only
thing we all agree on is that we don't have one. Yes, hybrid cars
help, and so will ethanol and renewable energy resources, but
these are just a start. They barely make a dent in our ravenous consumption of oil. An industrialized society (as the Chinese are rapidly discovering) has a huge ripple effect on the quality of air. The
U.S. refused to ratify the Kyoto accords on global climate change,
although we're the world's biggest polluter on a per capita basis.
We proposed no realistic alternative to the latest international environmental treaty. Again, we're a government defined by inertia.

Festering deficits, a poorly designed tax system, an addiction to oil (in President Bush's own words), and uncontrolled entitlement spending are all symptoms of what is wrong with our current politics.

And there are no solutions on the horizon.

The stock market has been robust, but the subprime lending crisis of the summer of 2007 has, at least temporarily, thrown the strength of the market into doubt, and raised at least the possibility of an economic downturn or perhaps renewed inflation. According to a *Washington Post* poll in the summer of 2007, economic pessimism is at a two-year high, and the *Post*'s Consumer Comfort Index (CCI) is stuck in negative territory. Moreover, the working poor, to a large extent, don't really have a stake in the financial markets. Most don't have 401(k) plans or pension plans. For those who do, the pension systems for most large corporations are contracting or collapsing. The middle class as we know it has begun to erode. Good jobs are being exported to India and Asia, fattening corporate profits and leaving unemployed and underemployed Americans bewildered. "The working class has taken a beating," said Ed Taylor, a pipe fitter from Topeka, while holding a protest sign proclaiming the need for more jobs. "Personally, I don't see the economy as strong as the numbers coming out of the federal government." The situation of the workforce will likely get worse.

The American Dream—that is, providing all Americans with the chance to achieve their goals and aspirations—appears to be becoming more elusive than achievable for most citizens. I discovered this firsthand when I conducted a survey for the Aspen Institute. Here are some of its key findings:

- Today, 61 percent of Americans say they are not living the American Dream.

- 61 percent of Americans who aren't living the Dream say they do not believe that they will ever achieve the American Dream in their lifetime.

- 75 percent say the American Dream is no longer realistic, with just one in four saying it is "alive and well" today.

- 9 in 10 Americans agree that it is harder to achieve the American Dream than ever before.

Is there any question that Americans are dissatisfied with their current government?

Once, the independent voter was considered an anomaly, someone who wasn't decisive (or comfortable) enough to be aligned with either party. Independent polling organizations have reached similar conclusions over the years. Now, many independents realize that neither the Democrats nor the Republicans alone have the capability to solve the nation's problems. And independents are in a fast-growing category, the one that eschews the notion of red and blue pigeonholing.

While the two parties disagree on many issues, on the biggest of all—who should have access to power—they are in perfect harmony: themselves and no one else. For the past century and a half, their efforts to erect a daunting maze of obstacles and challenges to any potential competitors have been remarkably successful; not since the 1850s, when the Republican Party was created, has the essential nature of the system changed. Yes, our system is rigged against third parties. If the Democratic and Republican parties were businesses, their leaders would be under investigation for illegally constraining competition.

While third-party movements and candidates have periodically emerged to challenge the status quo—Teddy Roosevelt in 1912, Henry Wallace and Strom Thurmond in 1948, George Wallace in 1968, John Anderson in 1980, Ross Perot in 1992—none have ever come close to winning, though they did end up having a significant impact on policy formation as a result of their campaigns.

The last three independent efforts, however, garnered more support than anyone realized, and the evidence shows that if voters had a clear sense that a third-party candidate could actually win, support would surge as election day approached.

I believe that there is the potential for that to happen this year.

I have worked behind the scenes in American politics for more than thirty years. As a professional pollster and statistician, I can read the responses and spot trends that others may not readily see. It's my view that the public confusion and frustration over the plain vanilla candidates is real, not really understood, and probably far greater than most political analysts believe. I'm also an analyst. I get out there and talk to people in the small towns of America's hinterlands. I've stood on their doorsteps, and I understand *how* people make up their minds on which candidates they're going to vote for. I've done countless focus groups, and I know how people think.

Identifying trends is my life and my livelihood.

I'm not naïve; in fact, I'm very realistic. I understand the odds are stacked against those outside the two-party system. Third-party bids for the White House have never succeeded. Ralph Nader failed twice under the Green Party banner and once as an independent; independent Ross Perot fell short twice; John Anderson's independent candidacy was unsuccessful in 1980, as was George Wallace's in 1968. Strom Thurmond ran and lost in 1948.

Yet today, for the first time in my three decades in electoral politics, I see something absolutely new: a real opportunity for an independent presidential candidate to emerge and win office—and not at some hypothetical point in the future.

Through either a new third party or a purely independent ticket, I believe that a nontraditional path to the White House is wide open.

History has shown repeatedly that third-party movements form when some basic conditions are met:

- First, the electorate is dissatisfied with the state of the country and believes it is on the wrong track. The executive branch and Congress are at close to record-low levels of popular approval.

- Second, a large segment of the American people thinks the system cannot be fixed. They just think it doesn't work.

- Third, the two major political parties are unpopular and the electorate is polarized.

- Fourth, the American electorate experiences the stress of economic uncertainty.

- Finally, America's image in the rest of the world suffers because of military intervention in foreign nations.

All of these conditions prevail today.

Moreover, as in 1992, when Ross Perot emerged apparently from nowhere, the general dissatisfaction voters feel is being exacerbated by the sense that key concerns are being ignored by both parties. Voters of the left and the right have now come to believe that neither side is willing or able to address seemingly unrestricted illegal immigration and the loss of jobs and economic opportunities overseas. Now that we are facing a potentially serious economic downturn, voters of both parties remain concerned that we are preoccupied with what appear to be intractable international conflicts at the expense of the domestic economy.

Of course, serious obstacles to a third-party candidacy remain. It helps to have access to significant resources. In January 2007, former Federal Election Commission (FEC) commissioner Michael Toner predicted that the 2008 presidential race will cost the winning candidate $1 billion, making it the most expensive election in American history. (In 2004, the total spending for *all* candidates was just over $1 billion.) There have been estimates that presidential hopefuls need to raise $2 million *a week* during the early stages of a campaign (that is, six months or more before the primaries begin) just to remain viable. Realistically, a candidate needs $100 million just to reach the starting gate. It's the world's most expensive horse race.

Not surprisingly, the bulk of the money raised goes to the media buys. The simple and direct relationship between the growth of campaign spending and TV advertising can be seen in Figure 1.

That $100 million figure is not a typo, and the 2008 presidential election is sure to shatter the 2006 record. Two obvious conclusions: first, money still matters to a significant extent, and second, so does television. But these notions are rapidly changing. As more people use cable TV recording services such as TiVo, there will be a greater incentive to fast-forward through commercials, rendering them less effective. And voters quickly will reach a saturation point, where the bang for the buck will be distinctly lower than in the past. Other, more creative ways of reaching voters will almost certainly become more prominent. Viewers

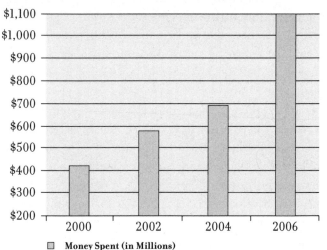

FIGURE 1. **Total Candidate Spending on the Top 100 Broadcast TV Markets**

☐ **Money Spent (in Millions)**

Source: TNS Media Intelligence/CMAG

will eventually go to ads they *want* to see—rather than tolerate those ads that are thrust upon them.

As we enter the new world of politics, it's clear that money isn't everything. Jesse Ventura, a former pro wrestler, upset two strong opponents, Republican Norm Coleman and Democrat Hubert Humphrey III, to become governor of Minnesota in 1998, and disproved the notion that it takes a truckload of Wall Street money to get elected. Ventura was ridiculed by the press and ignored by his opponents, yet he generated positive publicity through daily postings on his campaign website and through regular contact with a three-thousand-member e-mail list called Jesse Net. Ventura's campaign has gone down as the first major election in history in which the Internet boosted a candidate to victory. Other campaigns, big and small, prominent and not so prominent, have used the Internet to develop their candidacies, fund their campaigns, and build their support base.

But as a longtime political adviser, I'm also realistic. I know that there is a huge difference between winning a governorship or a Senate seat and being a successful third-party presidential candidate. The impediments loom larger.

Money, media attention, ballot access. These obstacles are not as insurmountable as most people think. Independent candidates in the past have mounted stronger campaigns than even many close observers of American politics realize. Moreover, advances in technology (delivered via viral marketing through the Internet) have lowered the hurdles erected by the dominant parties that have thwarted independent candidates in the past. Multimillion-dollar direct-mail campaigns—once the backbone of fundraising—can now, in some circumstances, be done instantaneously for pennies with a click of the mouse.

The Internet has made populism more popular and effective, giving power and sway to an electorate in ways nobody ever dreamed of. It can quickly build a national campaign organization.

There is no Howard Dean without the Net. Without the Net nobody would have known who he was. His was the first presidential candidacy created in cyberspace, but it will not be the last.

The power of YouTube, with its instant videos viewable by millions, has yet to be measured in a presidential race.

This change will continue because the notion of conventional media is long gone. Today, the Internet has fostered multiple news cycles in any given twenty-four-hour period. Every major daily, the networks, and cable news are now sensitive to the fact that their websites must be updated as events occur. If you surf the Web today, you'll note overkill coverage of every candidate, major or minor. There are at least half a dozen sites devoted to collecting petition signatures to draft noncandidate Al Gore in 2008.

The aides and advisers who run the campaigns are just now beginning to understand the Internet's power, its effect on the media and, ultimately, on the outcome of presidential elections. And because more people have access to advanced cell phones and PDAs, the impact of instantaneous communication is going to be even greater in the 2008 presidential race.

There is also another reason to expect a third-party run in 2008. The presidential campaign season is now a full two years long, twice the amount of time we used to have to assess candidates. (Recall that Bill Clinton didn't begin his first presidential campaign until October 1991.) This allows candidates to spend extraordinary amounts of money prior to the primaries. In the states that matter the most, the primaries have been pushed up on the calendar. Thirty states may choose their convention delegates by February 5, 2008. So there's a greater likelihood we'll know the party nominees early in the election year.

All this will open the field to a wide range of potential third-party challengers: a Democratic or Republican candidate who lost in the primaries, or someone from outside the primary nominating system, or other luminaries like Bill Gates, Steve Jobs, or a media personality like former news anchor Tom Brokaw. Businessmen are no longer considered political wannabes with big bank accounts. They're now taken seriously because they go beyond petty politicking and are known to "get things done." Or any other new face, for that matter. Former radio talk show host Al Franken is running for a U.S. Senate seat from Minnesota. He's a serious candidate with a very vocal following. Stranger things have happened in American politics.

At the end of the day—certainly at the end of the election season in 2008—the nation will have to confront bigger questions than whether an independent candidate has actively mounted a campaign for president. The larger question will remain: can the political system deal with the issues and challenges that created an opportunity in the first place for a third-party candidate?

What is important is that politics as usual will be a thing of the past. There is a new language of politics and new challenges to be faced. In 2009, pundits, analysts, and political advisers like myself—and certainly the new president's brain trust—will realize that the rules of the game have dramatically changed. Our leaders will finally understand that they have to realistically take on difficult challenges and swiftly confront them. In the future, staying safely on "message," waffling when it's convenient to mollify an audience or interest group, just won't cut it in running the government or in campaigning for office.

The electorate has made it clear that the main plank in any platform has to be sensible problem solving. You can sense this in every region of the nation. As former Maine governor Angus King, an independent, puts it, "The public doesn't care whether it's a Democratic solution or a Republican solution. They want the roads fixed. They want the schools to work. They want reasonable gas prices. And, if called upon, they understand the necessity of sacrifice. I think we have become somewhat soft and self-centered. But, I think if called up and led, people will do the right thing. The American people always have."

The future of America may not be determined by the Republicans and Democrats at the top of the ballots. The two-party system does not necessarily represent the best of our past. It need not represent the best of our future.

The emergence of a viable third-party candidate would be profoundly good for America. But just hoping for one misses my larger point, for this book is about much more: it's about the fundamental shift in the way Americans are thinking about their leaders.

They understand that the really difficult issues aren't about black and white, but about shades of gray. Most of us do not see ourselves as living in a Red America or Blue America. In fact, as think tank experts in both camps argue, the notion of a blue state or a red state is simply a fallacy, and it's a fallacy perpetuated by those who want to stereotype voters.

Ours is fundamentally a nation of moderates who want nonpartisan solutions to serious problems. Dividing us into red and blue Americas, as the current electoral system does, is unnecessary, counterproductive, and ultimately destructive. This book is about the fundamental changes that are occurring every day. It will be the first major work to analyze the large-scale trend that could open the door for a major third-party candidate. And it will also explain how the major-party candidates need to talk about the real issues facing the country, communicate directly with voters, and ultimately restore public trust in government.

DECLARING
INDEPENDENCE

2008: Why America Is Ready for a Third-Party Candidate

The right candidate . . . might be able to drive a bus right up the middle of the U.S. political scene today—lose the far left and the far right—and still maybe, just maybe, win a three-way election.

—THOMAS FRIEDMAN, *New York Times* op-ed columnist

THERE IS NO DOUBT THAT WE ARE AT A CRISIS POINT IN AMERICAN politics. The American people are increasingly developing doubts about the efficiency and responsiveness of our institutions. And these increasingly deep-seated doubts cut to the very core of our philosophy of governing. As a result, there is a crisis of legitimacy in our democratic system. Polls show it, focus groups resonate with it, and political columnists are reporting it day in and day out. The crisis is due to a lack of credibility in the system itself. There are record levels of cynicism about Congress and the president. Americans lack confidence in both major parties, and believe they are far too partisan; they squabble endlessly rather than working collectively and collegially to solve our most pressing problems, and act as if ideology matters more than the greater good of the citizenry.

As a result, we're where we were in 1992 in terms of the level of dissatisfaction that allows a third-party presidential candidate to emerge. But we're also at a point where the record level of dissatisfaction impacts directly and immediately on the overall functioning and, indeed, legitimacy of our system of government.

Frustration and unhappiness are subjective feelings, and they change all the time. But they are quantifiable feelings nonetheless, and are measured obsessively by research organizations. According to a Gallup survey taken in the middle of May 2007, there has been a sudden plunge in its regularly reported "Satisfaction" index. Only 25 percent of Americans now say they are satisfied with the state of their country. The index has dropped 8 percent in just one month, and is at one of the lowest points ever measured.

Three out of four people are dissatisfied with the way things are going in this country.

"The current 25 percent satisfaction level is very low by historical standards," according to the polling firm. "Since Gallup first asked this question in 1979, the average percentage of Americans saying they are satisfied with conditions in the country is 43 percent."

In June 2007 Gallup reported that the percentage of Americans with a "great deal" or "quite a lot" of confidence in Congress was at 14 percent, the lowest since the polling organization began taking this measurement—and the lowest of any of the sixteen institutions included in its 2007 "Confidence in Institutions" survey. It was also one of the lowest confidence ratings for any institution tested over the last three decades. The bottom line, concluded Gallup, was that "Americans are in a very sour mood."

David Broder, the *Washington Post* political columnist, interviewed California governor Arnold Schwarzenegger for an Outlook column published on July 1, 2007. Schwarzenegger had thoughtfully taken the pulse of the people. He said, "People want bold leadership, somebody who is clear in his or her views, who can make tough decisions and who will reach across the aisle to address the important issues—health care, immigration, public safety, climate change, and the rest—someone who has a vision and a plan for the future, well beyond the next election."

He went on to say, "Voters admire you when you are willing to talk about difficult issues. Politicians think you have to be careful when dealing with powerful interests, but really you've got to be daring.

"People are looking for leaders who can bring people together. If the parties don't provide them, then a latecomer can come in from the outside and provide leadership that will work on the problems," he concluded.

In short, we are facing a wide-open contest, ripe for a dark horse, including a third-party or independent candidate.

And if you think this is just a refrain from Ross Perot in 1992, think again.

Here are the results of a series of three Gallup polls, the most recent one taken right before the critical midterm election that turned around the House and Senate majorities in favor of the Democrats. The data show that the United States is now facing a similar level of dissatisfaction to that which it faced before the last two major independent campaigns for president, in 1980 and 1992.

The trend is clear: The voter satisfaction chart (Figure 2) shows that in three years during the past three decades—November 2006, November 1992, and November 1979—the great majority of Americans were unhappy "with the way things are going in the United States." At these peak periods of dissatisfaction with the system, the electorate demonstrated the greatest receptiveness to change. In 1980 we had the "Reagan revolution," along with Anderson's third-party run, and in 1992 Perot reflected voter ire as Bill Clinton ultimately ended twelve years of GOP rule in the White House.

FIGURE 2. **In General, Are You Satisfied or Dissatisfied with the Way Things Are Going in the United States at This Time?**

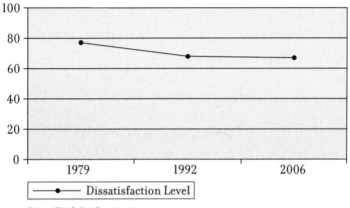

Source: The Gallup Organization

Today, the dissatisfaction level is virtually the same as it was sixteen years ago. Although the government's official numbers show solid and continuing growth in gross domestic product (GDP), public opinion polls suggest something quite different: an increasingly acute economic pinch among many working-class and middle-class Americans. The still relatively high level of the Dow Jones average does not accurately reflect what is going on in the hinterlands, where a substantial number of people struggle in low-paying jobs without health insurance. There are increasing concerns about high energy prices, the stability of the credit markets, and the impact of a falling dollar on the economy.

There are also serious issues apparent when we assess the economic well-being of all but upper-middle-class and wealthy Americans. This crisis has several specific components:

• Adjusted for inflation, real wages are stagnant and the better-paying jobs are hard to obtain.

- Americans fear they will lose their jobs to outsourcing, especially to India and China.

- Voters are concerned with rising costs in almost every area that matters to them: education, taxes, housing, child care, energy and gasoline, and health care.

- The long-term viability of Social Security remains a front-burner issue, as it has been ever since the Democrats raised the issue in the late 1990s and then George W. Bush took it up again after the 2004 election. The burden of retirement has also changed and it is now squarely on the backs of workers—a fundamental shift from past generations.

- The great American Dream of home ownership is becoming more difficult for many to realize. Housing prices have risen dramatically over the past ten years, notwithstanding the current softening of the market. Six in ten Americans say they are not living that dream. And many of those who are not living that dream feel they will never be able to live it.

- Subprime lenders are experiencing an increasing number of delinquencies and foreclosures as homeowners who took out adjustable-rate mortgages are facing higher and higher monthly payments.

Bottom line: Too many people have come to believe the American Dream is harder than ever to achieve and that the political system has largely failed to produce policies that improve their quality of life. Add to this the frustration they feel about America's image abroad, including our inability to solve the Iraq conundrum, and it's easy to understand why so many voters contend that we are a country in crisis and that our leaders are taking us in the wrong direction.

Frustration and unhappiness turn to anxiety and anger—and that's something the media and most politicians are slow to realize. But there's something bigger going on. The American people are clamoring to make a statement not just about individual candidates, but about the system itself.

Data collected by the University of Michigan's American National Election Studies reveals that the voters' trust in the federal government has plunged to historic lows. The electorate has doubts about the everyday issues, and added skepticism about the Iraq War. According to a research paper prepared at the University of Michigan, "The high levels of political alienation are unprecedented because they do not coincide with an economic downturn; instead, they appear to reflect widespread insecurity regarding the federal government's ability to resolve or otherwise cope with major problems confronting the country."

Along with this frustration with their leaders' failure to address their most important concerns, voters also have less confidence in their leaders' ability to solve any of the outstanding problems they do decide to tackle. Further, the American people also have come to distrust what their government is telling them. And according to the Michigan study, they are increasingly "more likely to support independent and third party presidential campaigns. . . ."

Americans sense that, in a changing world, the country's two main political parties are failing to recognize the gravity of our economic ills and seem incapable of providing the visionary leadership so sorely needed. People do not think of the leading Republican and Democratic candidates as "visionaries" or "leaders." They view them as adequate at best.

They see politicians in Washington, Democrats and Republicans alike, reduced to partisan bickering and name-calling, at the expense of substantive discussions about the vital issues we face as a nation. They see the world around them, and the economy they depend on, changing before their very eyes. Yet the parties' debates seem oddly removed from the nation's pressing problems. Instead of debating withdrawal plans for Iraq, our parties became preoccupied in fall 2007 with MoveOn.org's attack ad on General David Petraeus and Rush Limbaugh's comments about "phony soldiers."

A Pew Research Center study released in March 2007 revealed: "By a 62 percent to 34 percent margin, most Americans agree that 'when something is run by the government it is usually inefficient and wasteful'; this is the highest level of cynicism in a decade."

In 1980, when the Republicans took control of the Senate, and when Ronald Reagan defeated Jimmy Carter in a landslide, distrust in the federal government reached 73 percent. It had never before exceeded 70 percent. It's worth noting that whenever more than two-thirds of the public no longer believe what their leaders are telling them, then a historic partisan realignment typically occurs.

The 2006 distrust figure was 77 percent, which is close to the historic high-water mark. The Michigan study concluded, "The recent surge in voter alienation is quite dramatic. Just two years ago, in 2004, a bare majority of respondents, or 53 percent, said they trusted the federal government to do what is right most of the time or just about always. . . . Never has NES polling data shown such a dramatic collapse in trust in the federal government." Excluding the last two years, the period that showed the largest decline in trust was between 1972 and 1974, when the country was buffeted by Watergate, a recession, and the end of the Vietnam War. During that two-year period, the trust in the federal government decreased far less than it did between 2004 and 2006.

With trust in government at an all-time low for the last thirty-five years, it is not a surprise that we're looking for new leadership—that is, someone we *can* trust. Another salient point: The crisis in American politics and leadership is much worse than our elected officials suspect. While the misery index (how people feel

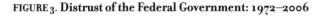

FIGURE 3. **Distrust of the Federal Government: 1972–2006**

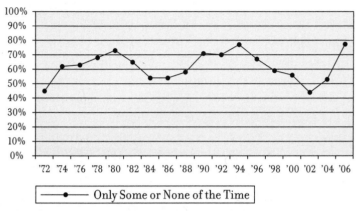

Source: American National Election Studies, University of Michigan

about their economic well-being, specifically their jobs and the increasing cost of goods and services) has remained fairly constant, people are more distrustful than ever. According to the Michigan study, "The current high levels of distrust have never before been present during a presidential election year. They are also exceptional because they do not correspond with worsening inflation and unemployment rates."

Other recently collected data support the conclusion of the University of Michigan. Pollster Scott Rasmussen has found that the approval ratings of a number of American institutions—the Democratic Congress, the Republican White House, and the nonpartisan Supreme Court—are all very low and slipping from levels recorded earlier. He has also found that the negative rating of the several leading presidential candidates—both Democratic and Republican—are growing across the board and on average exceeded 40 percent.

As John McCain said during a recent Republican debate, in effect summing up these findings, "The American people no longer have trust or confidence in our government. Our failure at Katrina, our failures in Iraq, our failures to get spending under control. And we've got to restore trust and confidence."

Americans look to third-party candidates when the two major parties appear unwilling or unable to accomplish anything positive. That was true in 1980, when John Anderson was at one point picking up 24 percent of the vote in public opinion polls against Jimmy Carter and Ronald Reagan; it was true in the late spring of 1992, when Ross Perot actually led in the polls, ahead of Bill Clinton and George H. W. Bush; and it is certainly possible for the right candidate in 2008.

Prior to the 1996, 2000, and 2004 presidential elections—and now, as we look toward 2008—about half of all Americans said they would like to see a third party join the Democrats and the Republicans in the political process.

FIGURE 4. **Some People Say We Should Have a Third Major Political Party in This Country in Addition to the Democrats and Republicans. Do You Agree or Disagree?**

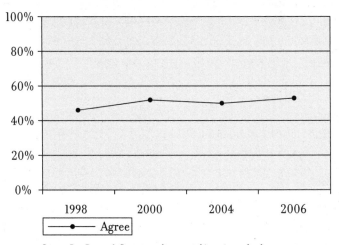

Source: Pew Research Center, results reported in various calendar years

For example, Fox News found that half of all registered voters in America think the formation of a third party is a good idea. The Pew Research Center found that 53 percent of Americans think we should have a third major political party in this country in addition to the Democrats and Republicans. Two separate polls conducted by NBC News and *The Wall Street Journal* found that slightly under half of all Americans would like to see the creation of a third party to field a presidential candidate. And a WNBC poll found that more than 40 percent of registered voters would be willing to vote for an independent candidate in 2008.

Thus, the polling results from several different sources are in agreement about the nation's views on the desirability of having a third-party contest in the next election. In addition, it is fair to conclude that America's divisive primary nominating system continues to produce Democrats who are frequently too liberal and Republicans who are just as frequently too conservative for the vast majority of American voters. The situation is all the more frustrating to the American people because candidates are forced to take left-wing and right-wing positions to get nominated, and centrists are almost by definition excluded from the process. The fault lies with the way the system currently works. Poll after poll shows that the American people are angry with political parties and supportive of a nonpartisan approach to politics and problem solving.

The intolerance of both political parties is equally clear and destructive.

For example, if you are a Democrat and support positions like school vouchers and free trade, the Democratic left will definitely think you are, at the very least, suspect. If you are not for immediate and complete withdrawal from Iraq, you are completely radioactive. Unless Democrats support left-wing positions virtually down the line and completely rule out initiatives like cuts in entitlement programs, they will have a difficult, if not impossible, time winning their party's nomination for president. The blogosphere demands as much, and it was no accident that all of the Democratic presidential candidates went to YearlyKos, the convention of the liberal blog the Daily Kos, in July except Senator Joe Biden (who was on his book tour), while they all avoided completely the centrist Democratic Leadership Conference (DLC) that same month, even though it was the DLC that was the intellectual foundation of Bill Clinton's presidency.

The same is true of the Republican Party. The Republican right has forced its presidential candidates to take extreme positions on abortion, immigration, gay rights, and gun control, and to put as little distance as possible between themselves and the failed Bush foreign policy. So again, as a Republican presidential candidate, you must adhere to right-wing positions on most of the social issues, as two former moderates—former New York City mayor Rudy Giuliani and former Massachusetts governor Mitt Romney—have awkwardly tried to do. As Kimberley Strassel has pointed out in *The Wall Street Journal*, posturing on immigration could well cost the Republicans the 2008 election. And no Republican will ever publicly support a tax increase during a campaign no matter what current fiscal conditions might require.

One alienated voter summed up this predicament nicely in a recent letter to *The Wall Street Journal:*

> *it is pretty tough to tell the difference between the Democrats and Republicans when it comes to spending. On top of that, while the Democrats' agenda still sounds like it is cobbled together from the pamphlets and websites of a hundred different left-wing groups, the Republicans appear more and more every day to march to the tune of the religious right. . . . It appears that this country grows more ready by the day for a third party that will meet the needs of the disaffected middle, those of us who aren't on the radical*

fringes of the left or the right. Maybe we should call it the Common Sense Party.

Not surprisingly, the "favorable" ratings of both parties are dropping, while the electorate's doubt about the ability of the political process to actually solve the nation's problems is growing. Poll after poll shows voters believe government, whether controlled by the Republicans or the Democrats, does more harm than good, wastes massive amounts of money, and serves the needs of special interests rather than ordinary people. Voters feel out of step with both parties and have a clear and overarching sense that the major challenges facing us are simply not being addressed by the Democrats and Republicans. According to a 2003 *CBS News* poll, voters want compromise and conciliation (83%) rather than parties that just stick to their guns (12%). And after the 2004 election, the Public Agenda Foundation concluded that almost three-quarters of the American people regarded compromise by our political leaders as a central, unachieved goal.

As Daniel Yankelovich has shown in a book he co-edited, *Uniting America: Restoring the Vital Center in American Democracy,* the American people do share common values and common goals. They have indeed rejected our divided political culture. Solid majorities of the American people support achieving common ground through core values like compromise, patriotism, community, and multilateralism. They continue to embrace policies that encourage hard work, respect for traditional values, and faith as well as individual liberty. Yankelovich rightly believes that the values we hold in common offer the basis for a set of policies that support this common vision. Coming from the perspective of a practical politician, Newt Gingrich has reached a similar conclusion, arguing that "the American people, regardless of race and party affiliation, are overwhelmingly united on key values and on the need for real change in the way America governs it-self."

Yet the extremist wings of both parties are drowning out the voices of reason and sensible compromise.

Rasmussen Reports, a highly respected electronic polling firm, tells us that in a survey of registered voters, independents have gone from 24 percent of the total in November 2004 to 32.4 percent in April 2007. People have been defecting from the major parties, but the number of Republicans abandoning their party is greater than the Democrats leaving theirs by a three-to-one margin.

Rasmussen's polling has revealed that 37 percent say they have voted for a third-party candidate or an independent in prior presidential elections. Some 28 percent say they have voted independent at the state or congressional level—indicating that the electorate is not necessarily as tied to the two-party system as many might believe.

The potential swing vote in American presidential politics is now more important than ever, with more and more voters either not registering as Democrats or Republicans or registering expressly as independents.

First, the American electorate is experiencing a surge in voters who identify themselves as independents. In the past fifty years independents have increased from one-quarter to close to 40 percent of American voters, according to Gallup polls.

Voters registered with either the Democratic or the Republican party are crossing party lines more often. Ticket-splitters—Americans who vote for a Democrat for president and a Republican for Congress, or vice versa—have gone up 42 percent since 1952.

In the 2006 midterm elections, self-described "strong" Democrats and Republicans each voted overwhelmingly (93 percent of Democrats; 91 percent of Republicans) for the candidate of their party, but it fell to independents (26 percent of the electorate, according to 2006 exit polls) to tip the balance.

Registered independents voted for the Democrat over the Republican by a margin of 57 to 39 percent, ensuring that the Democrats would take control of the House and Senate. Thus, the independents were the kingmakers of the 2006 election.

And there is more going on than just the number of nonaligned voters or independents increasing or independents simply making the difference in a number of key elections. There is a segment of the electorate that I have called the Restless and Anxious Moderates, or the RAMs, who I believe will decide the election. They include most of the independents and a fair number of Democrats and Republicans as well. These voters are practical and nonideological and unabashedly results-oriented. They eschew partisanship and want the parties to come together to confront the difficult challenges America is facing. Indeed, it is my argument that the RAMs could become the Restless and Anxious Majority if a credible third-party candidate emerges.

The RAMs make up roughly 35–40 percent of the American electorate, and they are fundamentally different from the partisans of the two parties. RAMs are ordinary, average Americans. They go online, they watch the news, and they are interested, but they are not the political activists of the blogosphere or the evangelical right. They are centrist, middle-aged, middle-class, practical people who believe in consensus solutions to problems. When they look at politics in Washington, they are aghast. They are looking for solutions that are outside the two-party system because they believe that the current arrangements are not working, are not producing results, and are not enhancing our democracy.

The Restless and Anxious Moderates, in my opinion, could grow to close to 50 percent of the electorate, should the polarization we have seen recently continue and the failure to address our pressing problems grow more pronounced. They have a number of basic principles about politics that can be summarized as follows:

> *"Address my life and the problems I face in my terms. Cut political rhetoric, cut political fighting, cut the game playing, stop the five-point programs. Just address my issues in a real-world, straightforward way."*

What the RAMs are saying is "We want to get on with it and move away from politics as usual." As Joe Rowe, a sixty-three-year-old lifelong Republican who is in favor of tort reform and privatizing Social Security and who now makes monthly contributions to Barack Obama's campaign, said, "You have to make a stand sometime, and there is so much more partisanship, and I would love to see someone who can be a reconciler."

In America's recent political history, there have been a number of times when the RAMs have been strongly motivated to vote for what they saw as nonpolitical alternatives. Probably the most logical and likely place to start is with Dwight Eisenhower in 1952 and 1956. He was able to rally the country as a commonsense centrist who pursued moderate social policies that enhanced and protected the New Deal, moved inexorably to address civil rights, and developed the Cold War consensus promoting a strong stance against Soviet expansion.

The next time the RAMs coalesced strongly was in reaction to Barry Goldwater's candidacy in 1964, when they overwhelmingly supported the election of Lyndon Johnson. Following the divisive campaign of 1968, Richard Nixon was able to rally the RAMs with his own appeal to the people he came to call "the silent center" or "the silent majority," who were middle-aged, middle-class people tired of the Democratic left's ideologically driven policies and supportive of what they believed were commonsense approaches to the problems facing them. In '76 a healthy percentage of RAMs saw Carter as the alternative to the failed policies and dishonesty of the Nixon and Ford administrations; Carter's plea for integrity and good government resonated strongly with them. And, similarly, in 1980 and 1984, Ronald Reagan was able to make the case to a solid majority of the RAMs that America needed limited government, a more optimistic worldview, and a stronger and more assertive foreign policy. Again this message resonated strongly with a dispirited electorate.

In 1992, it was very clear that with the nation in recession and the Bush policies having failed, the electorate was looking for change. However, with a divisive nominating process on the Democratic side and the lingering questions about Bill Clinton's personal life and draft status, there was a wide opening for third-party candidate Ross Perot and concern across the board about the budget, politics, and the deficit. The Restless and Anxious Moderates became close to a majority of the country during that election. And at the end of June 1992, Perot had up to 39 percent of the vote simply because of the outrage of this group.

The goal of the work that Mark Penn and I did with President Clinton beginning in '94 was to get the Restless and Anxious Moderates of 1992 back into the Democratic column in 1996. It was very clear to us that three things had to happen. First, Clinton had to get rid of the perception that he was associated with the cultural and political left of the Democratic Party. Second, he had to demonstrate that he was still a fiscal conservative. Third, and probably most important, he had to show concretely that he was in touch with the values of ordinary Americans.

Because of health-care reform and his tax increases in 1993 and 1994, the public felt that Clinton was out of step with America. In focus groups I conducted in the run-up to the '94 election, voters said that something had gone wrong with Clinton—that he fell out of sync. And I can recall in early February of '94 being alone with Clinton in his private study, and Clinton said to me, "I'm out of position. Something's wrong. What's going on? I don't understand it. Tell me what's wrong."

"Well, Mr. President," I said, "I think a couple of things are going on. First, they see you as out of touch and out of step. They don't see you identifying with their lives."

"Yeah, I understand that. But something else is going on that I don't get," Clinton said.

"Well, let's be clear. There is a clear sense in America that to get elected you must be a fiscal conservative. And they perceive that you supported the largest tax increase in American history, and that hurt you."

"No, I know that. And I understand that we must do something about that."

"The only way to get their votes back," I told the president, "is to support a balanced budget."

I explained to President Clinton, clearly and repeatedly, that unless he was committed to fiscal discipline and to a balanced budget, he was not going to be reelected. I had seen it in elections consistently, most notably in Indiana when I helped elect Evan Bayh to the Senate (he was governor at the time) in the reddest of red states: unless Democrats are perceived as fiscally prudent, voters will not listen to the rest of their message. That being said, a candidate or elected official who did appear to be in sync with the electorate's fiscally prudent message was much more likely to get a positive reaction to the rest of the message.

Clinton ultimately agreed with that. He was prepared and did take on the entire Democratic caucus in the Senate and in the House. Despite protests from his then chief of staff, Leon Panetta, that he would lose his supporters in both houses of Congress, Clinton was ultimately persuaded that he had to support a balanced budget and that he had to propose one, despite attacks he would receive from his own party.

But Clinton said, "There's still more to it than that. I need help." And help came from Mark Penn, who suggested that it was about more than just economics.

"Mr. President, you have to talk in terms that the American people think in. And that's not just economics, it's values," Penn said.

Penn was, of course, right: it was about both economics and values. But it was more than simply justifying support for Medicare, Medicaid, education, and the environment in terms of the values by which the vast majority of Americans live their lives. It was also talking about issues in commonsense ways that spoke directly to the needs and concerns of the American people. Bill Clinton was criticized in 1996 and sometimes even mocked for taking on small issues like seat belts in buses, school uniforms, and so on. But at that time, those issues spoke directly to voters. They may have been small to the press, but they were important to the electorate. By talking about fiscally conservative issues in terms that Americans understood—not only balancing the budget, but at the same time standing up for clean air and water, education for all, and medical care for the elderly and for the poor, Clinton was speaking to commonsense values. As soon as he found his voice, the Restless and Anxious Moderates swung dramatically in his direction.

In that election we referred to the RAMs differently: we called them Swing 1 and Swing 2. Swing 1 were the Restless and Anxious Moderates who already leaned toward the Democratic Party and were easily persuaded. Swing 2 voters were much more skeptical. They were more fiscally and culturally conservative, but still open and still rational; they rejected the orthodoxy of Newt Gingrich and the Republican right. The success of that campaign proved that we could turn around both Bill Clinton's image and the image of the Democratic Party. It was very clear that our approach worked extremely effectively.

We used a similar appeal in the 1998 midterm congressional election. Midterm elections are historically difficult for the party of an incumbent president, particularly one in a second term, to win. But 1998 proved to be different. Our slogan was "Progress, Not Partisanship," which spoke directly and fundamentally to the so-called RAMs because it said,

> *"Stop the fighting. Stop the attacks over impeachment because of Monica Lewinsky. Let's get on with growing the economy, protecting Social Security, enhancing education, and protecting the environment."*

It was a commonsense plea to continue the undeniable progress of the first four or five years of the Clinton administration.

In 2000, George W. Bush won back a healthy number of the RAMs with his support for "compassionate conservatism" and appeared to be poised to govern in a centrist, inclusive manner. Bush was aided by Al Gore's break with Bill Clinton's electoral strategy and his advocacy of a neopopulist "people vs. the powerful" strategy, which clearly cost the vice president the 2000 election. But instead of building on his 2000 campaign rhetoric to try to further unify the country after 9/11, President Bush let his coalition fray and let the RAMs move away from him in some degree as the 2004 election approached. A more inclusive approach by President Bush could well have led to a more substantial 2004 victory and higher levels of support for Republicans and the Republican candidates. When politicians speak directly to the RAMs in their language, they respond in enormous numbers. In earlier elections, people like John Anderson, Ross Perot, and even George Wallace have spoken to unaddressed, deeply held commonsense concerns and won high levels of support at least in part as a result of their perceived candor.

To be sure, the RAMs as a group are somewhat amorphous.

They don't identify themselves as RAMs and they certainly do not wear buttons saying, "I'm a Restless and Anxious Moderate." But if you talk to a sampling of these voters they will sound alike. They will tell you forthrightly that they are practical, have common sense, support middle-of-the-road policies, and vote for the man, not the party. They are deeply concerned about the role of special interests and corruption in government. They want to deal with social problems in a fiscally sound, prudent fashion; abortion and gay marriage are low on their priority list. While they certainly don't want to stay in Iraq and lose thousands of lives, they also do not think that the United States can walk away from the war on terror or the country's long-term commitments. While protecting our border is important to them, they do not think it is practical to send the 10–12 million immigrants currently in the United States home, and they are by no means obsessed with illegal immigration. The RAMs believe that we have a responsibility to deal with health care for our elderly and for our children in a fiscally responsible way. They say that we have to take on challenges such as cutting entitlements and raising taxes, and they recognize that we cannot do "business as usual"—we have to bridge the partisan divide because our quality of life is too important and it is at risk.

In-depth interviews with RAMs bear these conclusions out. I spoke in detail in September 2007 with fifty RAMs who fit the general demographic profile described above. Here are some of the responses I got when I asked about the two-party system:

> "Neither the Democrats nor the Republicans have helped the people enough. We need an independent who represents the people, not a party or a special interest."

> "It's all about one side 'always' believing this and the other is ultimately against it, without any gray area."

"No one can agree on anything. Each side is so worried about being right that they don't want to take the time to hear each other out and find a way to put the best of both parties together for the best of everyone."

"People are so entrenched with one side or the other they actively don't hear what the other side is saying."

A survey by *The Washington Post*/Kaiser Family Foundation/ Harvard University provides additional insights into the mindset of the group I have called the Restless and Anxious Moderates. I shall discuss this survey below. My analysis provides a different emphasis and different conclusion than the *Washington Post* report initially presented.

It is important to note at the outset that 29 percent of the survey respondents said that they were political independents, and it is this group that I am using as a proxy for the RAMs. An additional quarter of the sample said they were normally Democrats or Republicans but also acknowledged that there were times when they considered themselves independents as well. Thus, a majority of the sample (54%) were either pure independents or supporters of the main parties who could in some circumstances characterize themselves as independents.

A look at how the pure independents think shows that they are for the most part quite engaged in politics, but are more discouraged than encouraged by what they observe. They divide almost evenly on the question of whether there are important differences between the parties, with half saying yes and 47 percent saying there are not important differences. In addition, only 38 percent agree with the statement that the two-party system does a good job of addressing the issues that are important to people like them; 60 percent disagree.

Moreover, when asked to explain why they are independents,

the vast majority rejects the notion that they are not interested in politics. They make it clear that it is issues and candidates that explain how they vote, not partisan considerations.

A close look shows that while independents remain somewhat hopeful about politics, their dominant emotions are frustration, pessimism, and anger. Very few independents are inspired by or proud of the political system.

A more detailed look at the data shows that the independents are more frustrated and pessimistic about politics than the Democrats or the Republicans. They are angrier than Republicans and equally as angry as Democrats, and less inspired than the other groups. Independents, like Democrats and Republicans, reject emphatically the notion that our political system would be better off without political parties. And by a large margin, voters who

FIGURE 5. **Major Reason to Be a Political Independent**

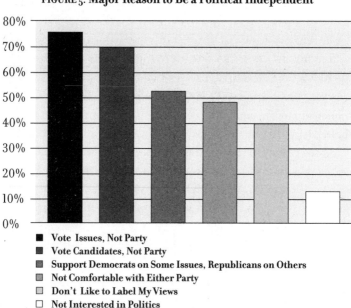

Source: *Washington Post*/Kaiser Family Foundation/Harvard survey, May 2007

FIGURE 6. **Independents', Democrats', and Republicans' Feelings About the Political System**

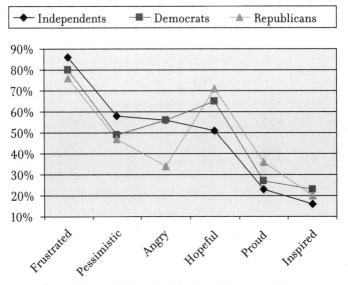

Source: *Washington Post*/Kaiser Family Foundation/Harvard survey, May 2007

identify with both parties and, especially, those who call themselves independents believe our system would get better, rather than worse, if it were easier for an independent to run for president.

When the *Washington Post*/Kaiser/Harvard survey looked at what independents want in the next president, the most important trait overall was integrity (48%). And while they want a strong and decisive leader (31%), they clearly consider it more important to elect someone who works on a bipartisan basis (31%) rather than someone who speaks his own mind regardless of the political constraints (23%). These preceding traits were vastly more important to independents than being inspirational (15%), having strong religious faith (9%), or having a lot of experience in elected office (8%).

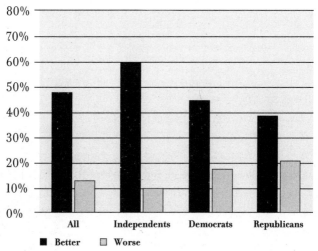

FIGURE 7. **System Better or Worse or Same If Independent Can Run for President?**

Source: *Washington Post*/Kaiser Family Foundation/Harvard survey, May 2007

Finally, the independents in the *Post*/Kaiser/Harvard survey said the war in Iraq (47%), health care (41%), corruption in government (39%), the economy (34%), and the campaign against terror (34%) were the top issues to them personally. Their second-tier issues were illegal immigration (28%), the federal deficit (25%), global warming (22%), taxes (23%), and social issues (17%) like abortion and gay marriage.

So while it is abundantly clear that a substantial percentage of the American people—perhaps even a majority—are seeking new alternatives, it is also the case that there are now methods and tools to channel that discontent which did not exist in prior elections.

As I outline later in the book, the Internet has created a more level playing field when it comes to grassroots organizing and fundraising.

The election of 2008 need not be a self-fulfilling prophecy. The final argument against a third-party candidate is that he or she can't win because no third-party candidate ever has. This observation is seemingly true but ultimately misleading. As I will discuss in detail in chapter 3, the last three serious independent candidates to mount aggressive challenges—George Wallace in 1968, John Anderson in 1980, and Ross Perot in 1992—all were surprisingly competitive in those campaigns for a much longer time than most now realize, as Table 1 shows.

Thus, George Wallace polled as much as one-fifth of the electorate as late as September 1968, despite being marginalized in the national campaign between Hubert Humphrey and Richard Nixon. Likewise, John Anderson's support as an independent candidate climbed from the single digits into the midtwenties in the spring of 1980 and stayed there through the fall of that year, despite the fact that he had drawn only limited support in the Republican primaries. Anderson drew an even higher level of support in the polls—usually 5–7 percent higher—when voters were asked to assume that he had a chance to actually win the 1980 election.

TABLE 1. Past Independent Presidential Candidates' Electoral Support

YEAR/ CANDIDATE	HIGHEST POINT IN POLLING	ELECTORAL VOTES
1992 Ross Perot	37 percent	0
1980 John Anderson	24 percent	0
1968 George Wallace	21 percent	46

Source: Harris, September 1968; *Los Angeles Times,* June 1980; CNN, June 1992

Similarly, Ross Perot began his seemingly quixotic campaign in February 1992 and quickly saw his own level of support jump dramatically into the midtwenties by the early spring and then to the mid to high thirties by early summer. Indeed, when he dropped out of the election in July 1992—temporarily, as it turned out—he was actually leading in some polls and some tallies of Electoral College votes. When he returned to the campaign in early October, his support had dropped back to the single digits. Still, with a compelling one-month TV campaign and an impressive performance in the presidential debates, Perot managed to get his support close to 19 percent. Exit polls showed that if voters had thought Perot actually stood a real chance of winning, his support could well have almost doubled into the midthirties.

Thus, a review of polling data from presidential contests in 1948, 1968, 1980, 1992, and 2000 shows that, contrary to conventional wisdom, previous third-party candidates for president had the potential to perform far better than was actually understood at the time. Though bogged down by impediments such as ballot access and difficulty raising money—and although in many cases their campaigns were poorly run—strong showings by these candidates highlights the willingness of the American electorate to support third-party candidates when the necessary factors are in place.

It is inaccurate and shortsighted to dismiss these candidacies as failures that validate the status quo. Consider the case of one of the weaker third-party presidential candidates, Ralph Nader in 2000. As late in the campaign as October, polls showed that as many as 16 percent of Americans said they had considered voting for him. Why didn't they? In part, because there was a ceaseless drumbeat from the mainstream media that Nader couldn't win, and that his candidacy played into the hands of George W. Bush. But had Nader been allowed to participate in televised debates— something Americans overwhelmingly supported—it's possible the entire dynamic of the campaign would have shifted. Nader could well have gotten around 10 percent of the total vote had he been allowed to fully participate in the 2000 campaign.

History has shown repeatedly that third-party movements have their greatest influence when three basic conditions are met. First, voters respond best to a third party when they are dissatisfied with the state of the country. That is, they respond best to third-party candidates when they believe America is off on the wrong track. Second, third-party candidates do better when the two major political parties are unpopular and when the electorate is polarized. Finally, third parties are successful when the American electorate is experiencing the stress and dislocation of economic uncertainty.

Even if a third party or independent candidate does not ultimately emerge this year, I would hope that politicians would take note of the following findings. Figure 8 clearly illustrates that the public is tired of the typical political cant reported in the nation's media about fundraising, polls, and political posturing. The implication is that the voters are a lot smarter than the media and most candidates are giving them credit for. (The media, after all, are for the most part reporting what the candidates are feeding them, week in and week out, during a campaign.) Specifically, the voters are not that interested in who is leading the fundraising race and they very much want to move beyond poll-driven reporting. They already know that half the money will be spent on TV advertising, with a substantial part of it during September and October of 2008.

In overwhelming numbers, they want the candidates to address the issues. And an overwhelming amount of evidence and historical data suggests that the third-party insurgents are the ones whose voices they would like to hear.

There are also procedural issues related to how the 2008 campaign has unfolded that makes the election of a third-party candidate more likely. The overly long primary process, with ever-shifting dates for individual state contests and close to ten candidates on each side, has hardly done much to pacify an already resistant electorate. Indeed, polls show that the electorate is getting increasingly frustrated with the whole undertaking on both sides of the aisle. As William Galvin, the Massachusetts secretary of state, recalled, "The country will see in this upcoming election that they have been left out. The rules for *American Idol* are more defined than these rules are." Indeed, who would have ever thought that less than four months before the actual primary voting was to begin in January, major Democratic Party candidates for president would have to advertise their willingness to actually boycott primaries in critical swing states like Michigan and Florida to show that they were in compliance with Democratic Party rules. It certainly isn't a net positive for the Democratic Party and its candidates to possibly have to boycott key primaries for internal party reasons.

Make no mistake: We have arrived at a historic moment. The

FIGURE 8. **Public Appetite for Campaign News**

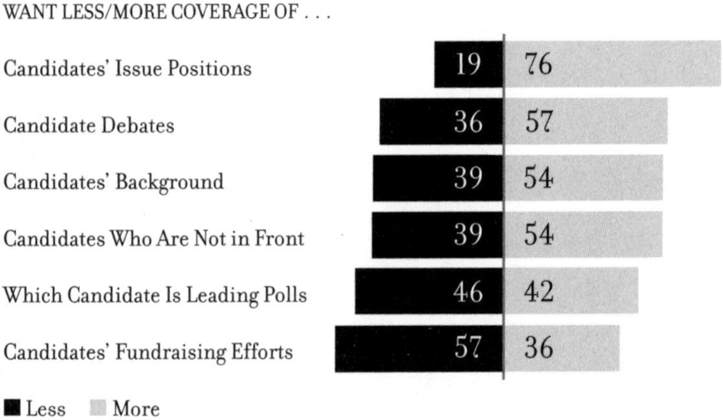

WANT LESS/MORE COVERAGE OF . . .

	Less	More
Candidates' Issue Positions	19	76
Candidate Debates	36	57
Candidates' Background	39	54
Candidates Who Are Not in Front	39	54
Which Candidate Is Leading Polls	46	42
Candidates' Fundraising Efforts	57	36

■ Less ▨ More

Source: Pew Research, May 2007

upcoming election could see an independent candidate successfully leverage the strong desire for additional alternatives to the
two parties and rewrite at least some of our assumptions about
politics as we know it.

As former U.S. senator Bill Bradley put it in his most recent
book, *The New American Story,* the voters deserve to have their ordinary expectations met by their leaders. "I believe that in a world
in which activists and political consultants focus on peripheral
issues—even in a world in which few elections are legitimately
contested and money seems a necessary evil—the political party
that emphasizes what 70 percent of the people care about will be
in power for a generation."

I agree with Bradley that the American people are anxious to
hear candidates delve into the issues that concern them and offer
realistic solutions to the problems that affect their daily lives. In
the next chapter, I'll discuss the problems that concern voters
most—issues that frequently go unaddressed in the way that many
would like to see them considered.

2

The Ideological Divide: Who Will Confront the Big Issues?

Like the Republicans [the Democrats] would rather play it safe than risk a genuine conversation about our future. What America needs in 2008 is the opposite of modern political campaigning.

—Former House Speaker Newt Gingrich

AS I WRITE THIS, WE'VE SEEN A REPUBLICAN DEBATE WHERE THE CAN-didates were asked whether they believed in evolution or creationism. Raise your hands, class, the moderator asked. The Congress has spent an inordinate amount of time arguing about the sexual orientation of soldiers. And there is more than ample discussion about the appropriate number of spouses a presidential candidate should have.

And the result is that all this is just white noise for most Americans. Voters don't really care whether there are gays in the military, as long as they're good soldiers. Voters are certainly capable of judging a candidate's qualifications and appeal without considering their personal lives. And ultimately, voters really don't care where we came from—the monkeys or some divine act from heaven.

We care about where we're going and how we're going to get there.

Bill Bradley wrote that "an inordinate amount of attention goes to issues such as abortion, gay rights, gun control, medical marijuana, the display of the Ten Commandments, the wording of the Pledge of Allegiance, or the subsidy desires of a particular corporation or industry—issues that don't motivate the majority but are all important to the activists."

Senator Jim Webb has articulated what may be a meta-issue of the next presidential campaign. There is a deep anger these days among middle-class Americans who feel abandoned by the elites in both parties. That anger surfaces on basic economic issues that affect working people—immigration, outsourcing of jobs, and the trade and tax boondoggles that broadcaster Lou Dobbs rages on about ad infinitum each night on CNN.

"The average American worker sits there feeling the impact of globalization and immigration. They need people sticking up for them," says Webb.

The in-depth interviews I conducted supported this conclusion. When I asked voters whether the presence of a third-party candidate would benefit the American political system, the answer was an unambiguous yes, and many voters understood that it would force the major parties to consider a broader array of policy options. Here is a sampling of the responses I got:

> *"It would put more issues out there. It would breathe more life into the stagnant agenda of the candidates."*

> *"We would clearly have a greater diversity of ideas and principles to debate."*

> *"We need some fresh blood and a new perspective on things."*

The parties are polarized but the people are not. It's almost incomprehensible to me that if some 65 or 70 percent of the people are in general agreement on a specific issue, we cannot come to some reasonable consensus to solve a problem.

There's an array of issues out there that just aren't being addressed by either party. The upper and lower houses endlessly debate issues that don't matter. What rarely gets addressed is what most people want: affordable health care for all Americans (now belatedly being taken up by both parties without any evidence of consensus), excellence in education, a Social Security system that will be there for them when they retire, a sensible immigration policy, a clean environment, an energy policy that can lead to less dependency on foreign oil, and an economy that generates more and well-paying jobs. You might even call them "postpartisan" issues.

Our divided electorate, as well as scholars such as Thomas Mann, a senior fellow at the Brookings Institution, believes that seemingly unpalatable solutions should be part of a bipartisan strategy that demands sacrifice from all. A third-party candidate has to rise to the occasion and raise these questions, and consider all the so-called unpalatable solutions. That candidate will win immeasurable support from a polarized electorate that is desperate for bold new ideas. It's going to take tough decisions to attack our most intractable problems, but more importantly it's going to take shared sacrifice, shared commitment.

Mann summed up the gridlock:

> *Remember, these are really big problems and they're really tough. Solving them is going to involve some major changes in the way we live, the way we tax ourselves, the way we get our health care and the way we transport ourselves.*
>
> *Many of these questions are caught up in ideological differences that really are quite fundamental. On all of them right now there is no consensus in the country and therefore the political system has to try to create one where none now exists.*

There are several so-called third rails in politics: Social Security (and private investment in the accounts), raising taxes, cutting entitlements and other benefit programs, raising the gas tax—things you don't touch if you're a politician. Republicans usually want to cut spending, Democrats typically don't want to see reductions in government programs for working people: nobody wants to say everything's on the table. Politicians don't want to be perceived as making the wrong choices, so they end up making none at all. All the hot-button issues are in stasis.

The labels are getting tired. "Tax and spend." "Weak on defense." They're broad accusations fired from either side of the aisle, and the result of it all is that few of our leaders are willing to confront the problems head-on.

What the American people are basically saying, however, is that you have to make the hard choices. If you take nothing on, then you've really hit the third rail. And polls have shown that people will pay more, they will accept cuts in programs, and they will do their part to advance the cause of the nation's business if they think the government is serious about effecting long-term, positive change. But if it's just political gamesmanship—which it appears to be—then they just won't buy it. There is no real bipartisanship. It doesn't work.

The American people, if the low ratings they have given both a Republican president and a Democratic Congress are a good indication, are convinced both parties have failed to successfully address the real problems facing the country. As Newt Gingrich has concluded:

> We've witnessed failure after failure of the permanent government: failure to secure the border; failure to adequately respond to Hurricane Katrina; failures in implementation in Iraq and Afghanistan; failure to control the grotesque explosion of congressional pork; failure to make our urban school systems produce ed-

*ucated children; failure to make English the official language of
government; failure to balance the federal budget; failure to fix our
healthcare delivery system; and failure to reform—Social Security,
Medicare, and Medicaid.*

*These failures of the permanent government are clearly unac-
ceptable to most Americans. But for the permanent government
and its interest group allies, the system works just fine because it
serves their needs.*

And so there is a wide range of issues that have to be taken up
by a third-party candidate. First, we need fiscal discipline. All of
the important subsequent issues emanate from our inability to
fund important items and spend less money than the revenues we
accrue. The federal debt has become something of a scandal. In
1992, the nation owed $4.1 trillion, and this figure has increased
every year. As of October 2007, it's more than double that number, more than $9 trillion, and growing every day. Much of it is
debt service, as we're borrowing money from foreign governments to cover the fact that we're spending more money than the
government takes in. It's the kind of simple economics and arith-
metic that Perot thrived on during his campaign.

The bulging federal debt, our failure to balance the budget,
and our dollar, which is weakening against other foreign curren-
cies, has produced a balance sheet that reveals we're going to be
perpetually in debt to the Chinese unless we take steps to reverse
the course. In 1992 foreigners held less than 20 percent of our
debt; in 2005 the figure had risen to 50 percent, according to research by the Concord Coalition. The fiscal problem also extends
to our trade deficits. We're importing more goods than we're exporting, and so we are running a large negative trade balance.

JOB GROWTH. As our manufacturing base has eroded over the last
generation, there are fewer and fewer good jobs available in the
U.S. If you're a blue-collar worker on an assembly line, and your

job at General Motors or Ford has just disappeared, or your job has been outsourced abroad, your prospects for future employment are dim. We haven't done an adequate job of shifting our job training and resources to an information economy. Many economists agree that official unemployment statistics and job creation figures, rosy as they have been, do not tell the whole story. Many jobs are temporary or seasonal, and many are low-paying positions in the restaurant industry.

As our economy relies more on information technology and the service sector, jobs have been going overseas. The help lines for American companies are being answered by people in Bangalore. To be sure, we live in an interdependent world in which certain tasks are better exported to other venues. We have to have free markets, and at the same time we can't just have pure free markets, so how do we find that balance? How do we encourage free trade while protecting American workers? This issue will eventually reach crisis proportions. How long can the U.S. remain the consumer of the world? The planet needs other customers.

In short, we need to make sure that globalization works to meet the needs of *all* Americans.

RETIREMENT FUNDING AND PENSIONS. We're a nation of spenders, not savers. Many in the workforce cannot afford to put money into various pension plans such as 401(k)s. So they're relying on the government safety net. Social Security soon will need a major overhaul. How do we preserve it? The system was implemented in 1935, and it worked very well for many years. But today, Americans are living longer and having smaller families, so there are fewer workers to support the growing number of retirees. It's getting harder and harder to sustain this entitlement. We're ignoring the simple math. By 2018 Social Security payments will begin to exceed the amount of money the system is taking in via payroll taxes. Nothing has been done to comprehensively address the long-term challenges to the system on a bipartisan basis.

We have to take this issue on in a bipartisan way. Do we raise the minimum benefits age? Do we institute means testing? Do we raise the Social Security retirement age threshold? Do we increase the pay-in rate on wages and salaries? Do we create a separate section of the nation's treasury to ensure there's enough money as we approach the second half of the current century? Do we have private accounts, as both the Clinton and Bush administrations have previously considered? And if so, how should they operate?

Also, what about military pensions? What about civil service employee pensions? Has anybody thought about how we're going to fund these steadily increasing line items? Instead of trying to answer these very important questions, we spent months debating just whether to privatize Social Security without considering all the outstanding issues facing the system.

HEALTH CARE. Though the United States arguably has the best health care of any nation, it is the best only for those people who can afford to pay for it. Health-care quality is uneven in many parts of the nation, and accessibility to competent treatment varies according to one's economic status. For far too many middle-class Americans health-care costs have been spiraling out of control. Part of the reason is that the cost of drugs has gone up dramatically. And advanced technology for modern diagnostics has big price tags. It's an issue that affects all of us—our children, our parents. Some 46 million people in this nation, including 9 million children, wake up each morning without health insurance coverage. They hope they don't get sick. They have to pay their doctors at the window, or rely on the emergency room at the local hospital even if they just sprain an ankle. Hospitals and paying customers have to subsidize this very expensive treatment.

Should we adopt a plan like the one in Massachusetts, which went into effect on July 1, 2007? It requires that every resident have coverage, with subsidized plans for the poor. Failure to comply will result in penalties on tax returns. Prescription drug coverage is to follow. Maybe the Massachusetts plan is not the be-all, end-all solution, but at least that state did something. Shouldn't we include this approach in the national debate?

During the Clinton administration, there was an honest attempt to address this problem, but the proposals fizzled because lawmakers felt the White House wanted to make sweeping changes that the taxpayers couldn't afford. Others were worried that we were headed toward a federally mandated single-payer plan. But how can we now find a way to promote a healthy society? Doesn't our workforce demand it? It's as if we just gave up on the issue except for a feeble effort to provide senior citizens with subsidized drugs under Medicare. Nobody is quite sure how effective this program has been. Our population is graying, and end-of-life health-care costs are skyrocketing. Medical care at the end of life consumes 10 to 12 percent of the total health-care budget and 27 percent of the Medicare budget. We need a plan, and our politicians have been avoiding the hard work of formulating one. And soon we'll have to pay the piper.

ENERGY, THE ENVIRONMENT, AND GLOBAL CLIMATE CHANGE. Tree-hugging has suddenly gone mainstream. Here is an issue where the people are clearly ahead of the politicians. In fact, even corporate America, which has made overtures to government officials about setting tougher environmental standards, is ahead of our politicians. (Can anyone remember the last time businesses lobbied government for regulation instead of deregulation?) Here's why business leaders are advocating tougher standards: Evidence analyzed by a consortium of the world's leading scientists supports the notion that the earth cannot sustain the current level and growth of industrialization unless we make major changes in our policies on greenhouse gas emissions.

Even the few skeptics who disagree with these findings and believe the current global warming phenomenon is just a blip in an eon should still be mindful of what we're spewing into the atmosphere. The famed environmentalist Barry Commoner asks, Why add to it? On a per capita basis, the U.S. is the world's leading polluter. The Chinese are close behind, as their industrial base increases at an astronomical pace. The U.S., in outsourcing much of its production, is indirectly putting carbon emissions in the atmosphere in several parts of the world. Like it or not, we have some responsibility for air pollution in Shenzhen. The issue looms large, and it's a combination of global climate change, its effects on the atmosphere and the environment, and whether or not this country can achieve a measure of energy independence. All of these issues are interrelated and cross the world's borders.

What should be done about it? There has been considerable talk about raising gas taxes, expanding trade, imposing new taxes on carbon emissions, giving tax credits for alternative energy—all sorts of new initiatives. What about nuclear power? It works safely in France, yet in the U.S. we've de-emphasized this alternative ever since the Three Mile Island accident in 1979. New nuclear plants are not being built, and we haven't yet figured out what to do with the waste from spent fuel rods. Should we build wind generators? What about solar energy? How much should we invest in ethanol production? These are all issues that need to be considered absent partisan political considerations.

Very little has been accomplished. Our national government appears to be unresponsive. After all, we did not even attend the Kyoto meeting that led to a worldwide accord on emissions standards. The state of California appears to be more progressive in acting to reduce emissions than the United States as a whole. The private sector is waiting—almost demanding—federal action. "It's nothing less than embarrassing that three of the world's biggest oil companies are calling for tougher measures than the White House," said David Doniger of the Natural Resources Defense Council. Or even the Congress, for that matter.

IMMIGRATION POLICY. We need to come to an agreement on the immigration issue. This is a nation that was founded by immigrants, and it has a long tradition of welcoming the poor, huddled masses to our shores. Welcoming immigrants is part and parcel of the American Dream. Today, we have catchwords that define the controversy: social justice, racial diversity, amnesty, residency requirements. Are immigrants good for America? They have been in the past, and a majority of Americans still believe we should open our borders. But questions remain. How many immigrants should we admit? What kinds of immigrants should we admit? How should we treat immigrants once they are here? Recent public policy has been murky, but most people feel that our immigration policy has long been due for an overhaul.

We need a real bipartisan solution that recognizes that Americans want to protect their borders but also want to open up the country for people who want to come here, become taxpaying citizens, and contribute to our economy and well-being. We have 12 million people who are here, and they're living outside our legal system. The vast majority of these immigrants are Latinos, and most of the Latinos are Mexicans. We're planning to build a fence to monitor the southwest border between Texas and Mexico. There is little agreement on whether this is a good idea, or even if it's practical.

At this writing, the White House's immigration bill, introduced in 2007, had failed to win passage because of a lack of broad bipartisan support. Yet public opinion surveys that have been released since November 2006 continue to show majority support for immigration policies that include enhanced border security, workplace and employer enforcement, earned legalization for undocumented immigrants with a path to citizenship, and expanded visas—guest worker programs—for future immigrant workers and families. Why can't Congress pass an immigration bill when the majority of the public supports one? It's because special interest groups and ideologues have our legislators' ears—particularly those on the Republican right. Moderate America is ignored.

A NATIONAL SECURITY STRATEGY. We cannot succeed as a nation unless we have a bipartisan national security strategy. We will succeed or fail as one nation; we must come to consensus. We have to recognize the threat of terror and at the same time reach out around it. How do we do that? Our defense spending is expected to be $623 billion in 2008, more than the combined defense budgets of Britain, Russia, China, and India. We spend $40 billion on homeland security. Candidates are running on the "fear" factor: Elect me and the nation will be safe again. Elect my opponent, and I can't be responsible for another attack. The vast majority of Americans do not believe in hysterical overreaction, especially when we've invaded two countries in the last six years and sent troops all over the world, from Somalia to the Philippines, to combat terrorism.

Ever since 9/11 there has been a greater concern that we are vulnerable to another attack by terrorist groups, rogue nations, or other nonstate actors who are capable of building weapons of mass destruction. As the world's leading military and economic power, the U.S. is the most likely target of these terrorists and tyrants. Questions abound. How do we finally resolve the North Korean nuclear threat? And the Iranian threat? Also, how do we protect against dirty bombs from terrorists? And, finally, how do we guard our woefully underprotected ports?

On the other hand, Americans who have accepted the fact that they have to remove their shoes before boarding an airplane are also practical. They do not want to live their lives cowering in fear. And this brings up a corollary issue: we need a sensible foreign policy. After four years (and counting), the populace has grown tired of our endless foray into Iraq. The central question is, Where does America's responsibility in spreading free-world democracy around the world begin and end? Should it be limitless? Just how long should we try to resolve civil struggles in other countries? How much warfare can we afford to wage at any given moment? How much freedom can we impose—and pay for—in hostile areas of the world?

In debating this issue, the American people are mindful that our stature abroad has eroded. We do not command the respect in foreign countries that we're accustomed to getting. As the war in Iraq continues, the global image of America has slipped further, even among countries closely allied with the United States. In Spain, only 23 percent now say they have a positive opinion of the United States, down from 41 percent in 2005, according to a survey that was carried out in fifteen nations by the Pew Research Center. Even in Britain, Washington's closest ally in the Iraq War, positive views of America are only in the midfifties, down sharply from 75 percent in 2002.

At the same time, the American people firmly reject any move to isolationism. A poll Mark Penn and I presented at the Aspen Institute in the summer of 2007 clearly demonstrates that the American people firmly embrace an ongoing international presence and involvement for the United States. Democrats would be wrong to read opposition to the Iraq War as opposition to a robust American presence in the world, and continued participation in the war against terror. The American people are seeking a bipartisan, multilateral approach to the development of our foreign policy.

EDUCATION. We are the most advanced nation in the world, especially in technology. But there is a very real fear that we are losing ground to other nations, especially Japan and India, when it comes to innovation. One reason for this is our declining standards in schools. Other countries have longer school days and longer school years. We're just getting around to eliminating social promotion and improving test scores.

The American Dream depends on opportunity. And opportunity means opening the doors for everyone, regardless of their means, to better themselves through education. We started with "No Child Left Behind," and that's good. Many believe that the U.S. is losing its global competitiveness, and this can be traced to the fact that we're failing our students. People want affordable colleges for their kids. They want to see teachers rewarded for excellence. Past administrations have called for national academic standards and national tests in the public schools. In both cases, Congress rejected the proposals. One problem with minimum standards involves the teachers. Rewards and promotions for educators include incentives to get their students to achieve higher test scores. But as Steven D. Levitt and Stephen J. Dubner, the authors of *Freakonomics,* explain, this doesn't always work out. There's a built-in motivation for teachers to cheat on their students' behalf. Why? Because it makes everyone look good, even if the achievements are hollow. Ultimately, it's a solution that fails everyone.

Americans want equality—it is part of our constitutional heritage, after all—and they certainly demand it in their public schools. Many think that we need national mandates to ensure that every child can get a decent education, not just those in more affluent school districts. Right now, most of our public schools are paid for through property taxes, and this is where the inequities begin. In Mississippi, education spending per student is less than half what it is in New Jersey. Why should being born in the right state confer a competitive advantage on some, while being born in the wrong state imposes an instant handicap? It's an interesting question, and it leads to others. Should better teachers get higher pay? If not, then what incentives should we give to teachers to better educate our children? Where do we stand on vouchers for public schools, charter schools, and open enrollment?

Neither political party has adequately taken on the issue of college education. A bachelor's degree has become a necessity for achieving the American Dream. But ballooning costs of tuition have put this goal out of reach for many lower-income families who want nothing more than to give their children every advantage as they make their way in the business world. Even public four-year institutions are becoming very expensive. Both the current Bush and past Clinton administrations have proposed tax incentives for education, but these ideas went nowhere. Congress was not yet willing to pay for those incentives.

POLITICAL REFORM. This must begin with the campaign finance laws that have essentially corroded the electoral system. Today, voters have a dwindling confidence in the system and much less faith in government in general. Special-interest groups can dominate a party or a candidate by pouring more money into politics through a variety of means, from bundled campaign contributions to soft money to issue ads. As vast amounts of money flow into the system, costs skyrocket. Consultants, pollsters, the media, all demand more and more of a candidate's coffers. What President Lyndon Johnson observed some thirty-five years ago is even truer today: the system is "more loophole than law."

There is no consensus on a solution, but there are signs that citizens and some bold public servants are taking the lead with "clean money" campaign reform. Voters in three states—Maine, Arizona, and Massachusetts—have floated clean money proposals and passed reform laws. In June 1997, members of the Vermont legislature voted overwhelmingly to create such a system. Although each law is crafted to meet the needs of a particular state, all establish an alternate financing system that offers full public funding to candidates for state office who reject special-interest contributions and agree to campaign spending limits. We need to do the same for our presidential elections.

Here are the problems:

- Congress is compromised by the appearance or public perception of improprieties and conflicts of interest because of the private money used to fund campaigns.

- There are, in fact, actual conflicts of interest, large and small.

- Contributions do indeed facilitate access to legislators, and that access can translate into action.

- Lawmakers on specific committees regularly solicit contributions from groups they regulate.

- Elected officials must spend too much time on fundraising, an activity that they almost universally dislike, which takes time away from duties they much prefer, such as constituent service and policy making.

We have to break this cycle of lobbyists running Capitol Hill; we must create a fairer system that both parties support; and finally, we have to propose a solution that restores the public's confidence in the election cycle.

To be sure, many of these issues have been addressed by the various Democratic and Republican candidates for president. But they have rarely been addressed in a bipartisan way that puts all policy options on the table. If nothing else, the range of challenges facing America in 2008 requires that all candidates, no matter what their party, address these problems in a fundamentally different way.

3

The Historical Significance of Third-Party Candidates

The only way we get new ideas in the system is when third-party candidates run. Only when Ross Perot ran did they really change here in America.

—MARISSA P., a 45-year-old woman and political independent, Michigan, interviewed in September 2007

WE ARE AT A UNIQUE POINT IN THE HISTORY OF PRESIDENTIAL POLI-tics, and we arrived at this point because of three important third-party candidates: George Wallace, John Anderson, and Ross Perot, all of whom changed the complexion of the presidential ballot and did much better than most people realize. They proved that much of the skepticism about third-party candidates is wrong. The electorate welcomed their candidacy and offered its support.

These candidates all polled extremely well for a long period of time. But all three were hampered by the structure of a system whose built-in impediments kept them from realizing their full potential. Nevertheless, they registered strong support in the polls long after political pundits and the media had written them off. Those candidates would have done much better if impediments such as organizational difficulty, ballot access, fundraising, debate access, and lack of media coverage had been removed. I'll go into more detail about these problems in the next chapter.

These candidates shook the foundations of the two-party system, and they all appealed to a divided electorate, voters frustrated with a system stacked against any newcomers. George Wallace, John Anderson, and Ross Perot—I can't think of three independent candidates with more disparate political views—ushered in the modern era of challenging the status quo in Washington. The election cycles of 1968, 1980, and 1992 were all pivotal. More than any other third-party hopefuls, they paved the way for today's independent candidates.

Each man had a distinct impact on the direction of the country.

- Wallace was in large part responsible for whites moving away from the Democratic Party to the Republican Party and for the creation of the "silent majority" popularized by Nixon's campaign, with its emphasis on law and order and traditional values.

- Anderson helped bring the environmental movement into the political mainstream and developed new ideas to address the energy crises that faced America; he also advocated fiscal discipline and fiscal prudence.

- Perot was perhaps the most influential political hopeful of the 1990s; he was largely responsible for the balanced budget, a newfound respect for fiscal discipline, and, ultimately, budget surpluses.

Each of these three candidates changed the direction of the nation and was much more popular than was ever understood or appreciated. Wallace polled 20 percent or more in September of 1968. Anderson ran over 20 percent for virtually the entire period from March until June of 1980, although he had ballot access issues, lacked a stable source of funding for media or organization, and didn't have a consistent message. Even at the end of the summer and early fall, when his general election campaign was in complete disarray, he was still polling between 14 and 18 percent. Anderson only managed to become competitive in two Republican primaries, Massachusetts and Vermont. Everywhere else, he ran further behind, and he even lost his home state of Illinois to Ronald Reagan. Yet the power of his potential appeal as an independent catapulted him to national prominence and led him to enter the campaign as an unaffiliated candidate. Perot led the 1992 race from March until July, when he dropped out. He reentered the race with 9 percent in early October, and because he did well in that month's debates, he ultimately received close to 20 percent of the vote.

The data were very clear from both 1980 and 1992. If the electorate had ever believed John Anderson or Ross Perot could actually win their respective contests, their vote totals would have soared and exceeded the level of support in public opinion polls. Anderson always polled 5–7 percent higher than his actual level of support if voters thought he could actually win the 1980 election and their vote wouldn't be wasted, and even at the end of the contest, the electorate saw him as far more compelling and competent a leader than his vote total reflected. For Perot, the exit polls after the 1992 election told a similar story. They showed that his vote total would have almost doubled to 36 percent if the electorate thought he had a real chance to win.

Anderson never really had a realistic chance to win. But the real lesson is that he did so well anyway. The level of dissatisfaction with the two parties and their nominees in early to mid 1980 was such that he polled as high as 24 percent at one point. From March through September he was polling between 16 and 24 percent. He did well in the first debate with Reagan, when Carter failed to show. When the League of Women Voters ousted him from the decisive final debate with Carter and Reagan, Anderson was marginalized by the press and his candidacy was dealt a fatal blow, causing his vote to drop into single digits.

Perot was a much stronger candidate than Anderson, but he never really had a serious chance either. Again, the miracle is that he did so well, especially after he dropped out and then returned to the campaign at the eleventh hour. Perot came along during a crisis with the budget deficit, plus an economy mired in a recession. He spoke about economic revitalization, balancing the budget, and protecting America. He wanted to rid the nation of wasteful spending as well as reduce the size of government. Perot had no political background, no real record in public, no serious vice presidential candidate, and no well-developed organization. And yet the polls showed him in the lead until he dropped out of the race in July.

Perot had significant ballot access challenges that occupied his campaign until mid-September, but the American people eventually got him on the ballot in fifty states. He didn't face funding issues, but he didn't run much of a campaign until his infomercials began airing in October. Despite his minimal effort and the challenges he faced as an independent candidate, he still ended up with close to 20 percent of the vote.

Even George Wallace, who never had a chance either, still received 13.5 percent of the vote. (In September 1968 he was running as high as the midtwenties.) Wallace would have done a lot better if his running mate hadn't imploded on national TV. When former general Curtis LeMay said that we should be prepared to use a nuclear bomb in Vietnam, it meant the beginning of the end for Wallace as a serious candidate. Through the 1972 campaign, Wallace still did very well in the polls as a prospective independent candidate, even though he was close to death after a May 15 assassination attempt while he was campaigning for the Democratic nomination. Nixon may well have ensured his own victory in the general election of 1972 when his administration chose not to audit Wallace's taxes and Wallace himself opted not to run as a third-party candidate.

Contrary to what most people know, there's a long tradition of third parties and independent candidates in America who have actually had a great deal of impact. And without them and the precedents they set, we would have no Bernie Sanders, no Jesse Ventura, no Angus King, no Lowell Weicker, no Walter Hickel, and no Joe Lieberman.

Lieberman, Weicker, Hickel, Ventura, Sanders, and King have demonstrated that you can win at least congressional and guber-natorial elections as an independent. The history—175 years long and counting—of insurgents, spoilers, renegades, and wannabes pushing their way onto state ballots is part of this nation's rich tradition of representative democracy. It is about those who want to change the course of the nation by participating in an uncon-ventional way. And today, their prospects are better than ever.

Unless you're a historian, you may never have heard of William Wirt, who in many ways was our first Ross Perot. Wirt made his mark as something of a father to presidential third-party candidates by running as the candidate of the Anti-Masonic Party in the 1832 election. Wirt, however, had a problem: he had previously been a Freemason and hadn't sufficiently denounced his past. His campaign was hamstrung by what must have been the ultimate flip-flop of its day, and he managed to win less than 8 percent of the nation's popular vote (though he did carry Ver-mont and its seven electoral votes). Andrew Jackson handily de-feated Henry Clay in that election.

The Anti-Masonic Party lasted less than a decade—its parti-sans were folded into the Whigs—but it had a major impact on American national politics. The Anti-Masons chose their candi-date through an open national convention, a radical idea for a time when the smoke-filled backroom was the norm. After the election of 1832, every major party—the Democrats, the Whigs, and the Republicans—opened up their nominating process as well.

From that point to just past the middle of the nineteenth century, third-party activity mainly centered around the Liberty Party and the Free-Soilers, both of which built on an antislavery platform, and the powerful American Party, more commonly called the Know-Nothings. The Know-Nothings were predominantly anti-immigration and anti-Catholic, believing that only American-born Protestants had the divine right to responsibly run the nation. The Know-Nothings operated furtively, though they developed substantial power in the Congress, gaining somewhere more than 18 percent but less than 30 percent of the House by 1857. (Because of their secretiveness, it's impossible to put a definitive number on the seats they controlled at the time.)

The second half of the nineteenth century saw a plethora of third parties that included the National (or Greenback) Party and the Prohibition, Union Labor, and Populist parties. The roster of presidential candidates from these parties was decidedly undistinguished, however. Not until the dawn of the twentieth century did the Socialist candidate Eugene V. Debs make the first of five presidential tries, none of which aroused more than small segments of the electorate in a serious way.

Theodore Roosevelt was the first to have a real impact on third-party politics in the United States. He ran in 1912 as a former president, and the circumstances of his candidacy were distinct from those of other third-party hopefuls. After he lost the Republican nomination to Taft at the national convention (despite respectable showings in the primaries), his supporters seceded from the party and decided to hang out a banner under the name of the Bull Moose Progressives.

The timing was not in TR's favor, however. The Progressives didn't actually form their party until after the filing deadlines in most states had passed, and the picture is made fuzzy, bordering on obscure, by the fact that in many states voters were voting not for candidates but for individual electors, who were often on the ballot by name without reference to which presidential candidate they were supporting. The bigger problem facing Roosevelt was that he split the Republican vote with Taft, making Woodrow Wilson's election all but inevitable.

In the end, Wilson easily won the 1912 election with a substantial plurality of the popular vote, but Roosevelt beat Taft by four percentage points, 27 percent to 23 percent, indicating that TR still held a strong appeal from his days as a war hero, big-game hunter, and conservationist. Eugene Debs, the Socialist Party candidate, received 6 percent, the party's best showing.

Despite the advent of World War I, the Jazz Age of the 1920s, and the stock market crash in 1929 that was a prelude to the Great Depression, third-party politics remained fairly fallow until midcentury.

One insurgent stood out during this era. Robert La Follette carried the third-party flag in the name of the Progressives during this time, but he represented a small minority of antimonopolists and farmers in the Midwest. From the late teens through the election of 1924, "Fighting Bob" or "Mr. Progressive," as his supporters knew him, was a virtually lone voice arguing that big business interests were coming to dominate politics. La Follette had sought the Republican nomination for president in 1912, but he was rejected and left the Republican Party. La Follette joined the Progressive Party and in 1924 wrote the platform for a consortium representing labor, farm, liberal Christian, and third-party groups called the Conference for Progressive Political Action, or CPPA. The 1924 campaign stands out because the Socialist Party joined with the CPPA advocates for their first and only joint run for the White House.

La Follette's campaign was underfinanced, and he finished in third place, but his showing was anything but embarrassing. He received 17 percent of the popular vote (Coolidge had 54 percent; Davis 29 percent), and he ran second in eleven midwestern and western states. He did win the thirteen electoral votes from his home state of Wisconsin.

By 1948, a restless electorate had begun in earnest to abandon the tradition of the two parties, on both sides of the political spectrum. This was the year of the famously narrow Dewey-Truman contest, but third-party aficionados will recall it more for the emergence of Strom Thurmond and Henry Wallace, two candidates at opposite ends of the political spectrum.

Wallace's résumé included the vice presidency in FDR's third term, and also cabinet posts as secretary of agriculture and secretary of commerce. He was the Progressive Party candidate, a staunch liberal who minimized the importance of the impending Soviet threat. The nation was moving in the opposite direction, assuming the hard-line, anticommunist stance that Richard Nixon would soon popularize and claim as his primary issue. Henry Wallace himself was soft on the Soviets at precisely the wrong moment in history, and it hurt his campaign. He squandered the early popularity that had led some observers very early in the campaign process to believe he could be a serious candidate.

Thus, Henry Wallace and the liberals did not dominate the insurgent scene in that election year. That role was instead played by the South Carolina governor Strom Thurmond.

Almost nobody today recalls the name of the States' Rights Democratic Party, but history buffs remember its followers as "Dixiecrats." Thurmond became the Dixiecrats' candidate, and though his bid for the Oval Office was as much of a long shot as Wallace's, the Dixiecrats were significant in one respect: they signified the beginning of the end of the "Solid South," a long-time bastion of consistent Democratic support.

Thurmond campaigned on a platform of preventing and resisting any federal attempts to end segregation and poll taxes, claiming that antilynching laws were unnecessary. Support for the Dixiecrats was strong in the Democratic machines of several southern states. The state Democratic Party in Alabama replaced the Truman ticket with Thurmond's, wiping the incumbent from the ballot. In Louisiana, Mississippi, and South Carolina, Thurmond was endorsed and Truman relegated to third-party status. The States' Rights Party was listed as a third party on the ballot in thirteen other states.

On November 3, 1948, *Chicago Tribune* subscribers woke up to the headline "Dewey Defeats Truman," but in the rest of the country incumbency reigned. Truman was elected to a full term as president, with 49.6 percent of the popular vote and 303 electors, even though he'd lost four states (Alabama, Louisiana, Mississippi, and South Carolina) to the Dixiecrats. Strom Thurmond's popular vote was only 18,000 more than Henry Wallace's; they each had 2.4 percent of the popular vote nationally. Wallace gained no electors, however, while Thurmond won thirty-nine. Half of Wallace's 1.16 million votes had come from the New York City region.

Two decades later, in 1968, a southern Democratic governor, George Wallace, mounted an independent candidacy that appealed directly to southern whites of all types as well as a substantial number of working-class whites in northern cities and blue-collar suburbs.

Wallace, who famously clung to the concept of a segregated South, ran as a candidate of the American Independent Party, which was founded in reaction to the 1960s counterculture. George Wallace's appeal was broader than Strom Thurmond's as he campaigned on race, class, and cultural issues. He framed himself as a populist, and developed an image as an "outsider" who defended states' rights, was tough on law and order, and stood up against the elites for the commoners. He was an aggressive campaigner, not afraid to speak his mind, and he engendered far more support during the 1968 campaign than many in the media ever realized.

The Wallace campaign knew that lack of ballot access was a huge hindrance in challenging the status quo, so it hired a team of attorneys to tackle the problem full-time. The campaign managed to get his name on the ballots in all fifty states (only the District of Columbia, with its large African American population, balked), but it took a Supreme Court decision to get him on the Ohio ballot by overturning an earlier defeat in a state court.

Not surprisingly, Wallace tapped into a vein of voters disenchanted with both Nixon and Humphrey. In September 1968 he reached his peak in popularity, with a polling number of more than 20 percent. As has been noted, his popularity did not last, almost certainly in part because of his hawkish running mate, former general Curtis LeMay.

Despite the effect of General LeMay, Wallace ended up with nearly 10 million votes (13.5 percent) and 46 electoral votes (all in the South), the best third-party showing since Robert La Follette in 1924. Wallace almost certainly took more votes away from Nixon than from Humphrey, making the election much closer than most expected it to be. Wallace's most important impact might have been that he exposed a raw nerve in the American electorate. People were unhappy with both major parties in 1968; they wanted someone to stand up for ordinary people. And he proved for the first time in the modern era that a candidate with a cause could get on the ballot as an independent.

Four years later, Wallace again ran for president, this time as a candidate for the Democratic Party nomination, but his bid was cut short by an assassin's bullet in Maryland. Though he survived, he was confined to a wheelchair as a paraplegic, and this effectively ended his presidential aspirations. There's no telling how well he would have done that year; he had won the Florida primary by carrying every single county. He was the Democrats' choice in Maryland, and he defeated George McGovern and Hubert Humphrey handily in the Michigan primary, gaining 51 percent of the vote. He was polling 18 percent as an independent even after he was shot.

George Wallace, more than any other single figure, was responsible for changing southern politics. He was largely responsible for breaking the Democratic Party's hold on southern whites, and facilitated many Middle Americans to support Richard Nixon and ultimately Ronald Reagan. Despite his rhetoric—it's difficult to imagine any scenario in which he could have won the presidency—there are few American politicians who have had as much influence on American politics.

The hostage crisis in Iran, a shrinking dollar, high prices at the retail checkout counters, and long waits at the gas pumps led to a general frustration among the electorate as the 1980 election approached. It was the perfect setting for John Anderson to emerge. When Anderson began to consider a presidential run, it was four years after the end of the Vietnam War and only five years since the resignation of Richard Nixon. Nationally, 45–49 percent of voters identified as Democrats, 22–25 percent as Republicans, and a remarkably solid 26–27 percent as independents. *Half of all voters under thirty were registered as independents.*

Anderson decided to go after the Republican nomination outside of the normal party structure. Anderson and his handful of determined aides knew their first task for an Illinois congressman with minimal name recognition was to test the waters to see if his centrist policies and his quirky, Cassandra-style "I'll tell you the truth" approach would fly.

The Anderson campaign moved slowly at first, both in gathering grassroots support and in fundraising. By September 1978, only $300,000 had been taken in, a fraction of what his opponents had already banked. In contrast, George Bush was bringing in $50,000 a night at fundraisers, and reported a total of $1.5 million to the Federal Election Commission by mid-1979.

As a Republican contender in the primaries, Anderson gained early credibility and some notice. In the winter of 1980, he was off to a good start. He finished a surprise second in the Massachusetts and Vermont primaries, although he lost to Reagan in his home state of Illinois. He was third in Wisconsin. Despite these modest successes he had low levels of support in Republican trial heats. Yet he was developing ever broader national support because of his fiscal conservatism and his support for environmentalism as well as a national energy policy.

For example, in an ABC News/Harris poll taken during the last week of April, respondents were asked, "Now, if you had to choose between Ronald Reagan, Jimmy Carter or John Anderson, which one do you feel would be a better leader in the White House?" The results:

37 percent for Reagan

31 percent for Carter

22 percent for Anderson

(10 percent preferred none of the three or weren't sure)

Though Anderson was clearly behind, this was a remarkably respectable number for someone most Americans outside his home state had heard little about. He still had much less visibility than either Reagan or Carter, yet more than one out of five voters said they'd prefer him in the White House. Such findings led Anderson to take the bold step in the spring of 1980 of entering the presidential election as an independent candidate.

Despite his growing attractiveness as a viable independent candidate, Anderson had serious problems that consumed his staff's time and energy. Probably the most serious problem Anderson faced was ballot access. By the time he announced as an independent, he had already missed filing deadlines in five states: Ohio, Kentucky, Maine, Maryland, and New Mexico. In each one, the Anderson camp had to use the same tactics to get on the ballot: gathering the required number of signatures, complying with legal requirements, and then challenging the deadline dates as unreasonably early and thus unconstitutional.

Nevertheless, Anderson won very positive coverage from the national media, similar to what John McCain received with his "Straight Talk Express" during the 2000 Republican primaries. As Anderson's run began to gear up, his staff developed what became Anderson's signature proposal: a fifty-cent-a-gallon gasoline tax to reduce energy consumption, offset by a comparable cut in Social Security taxes. As a result of that proposal, known as the "50-50 Plan," Anderson was called "Courageous Candidate of the Year" by the *St. Paul Pioneer Press,* a characterization echoed by the national press. In his campaign memoir, Mark Bisnow, Anderson's press secretary, quoted *Chicago Tribune* columnist Michael Killian: "Anderson is candidly facing up to a serious unpleasant reality with an eminently workable if admittedly painful solution, just as he'd have to as president." The result was that Anderson won broad public support despite a weak campaign organization, continued poor fundraising, and ongoing problems with ballot access.

Consider Figure 10, a compilation of polling results of two questions asked of registered voters during a four-month period in 1980 when Anderson was an independent candidate.

Anderson was clearly a serious candidate. All summer long, he polled between 25 and 30 percent when voters were asked to assume that he stood a real chance of winning, and during two of those months he appeared to be running ahead of or neck and neck with Jimmy Carter.

Anderson's reputation for candor and integrity lasted a long

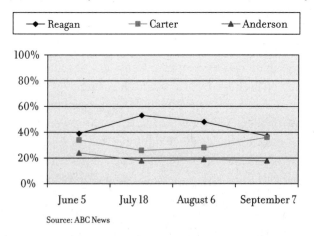

FIGURE 9. **If the 1980 Presidential Election Were Held Today**

Source: ABC News

time, even after his poll results dipped closer to election day. In September 1980, Gallup respondents saw him as a "decisive, sure of himself" (51%) candidate who "takes moderate, middle-of-the-road positions" (41%) and "says what he believes, even if unpopular" (46%).

FIGURE 10. **If Anderson Stood a Real Chance of Winning the Election, Would You Vote for Him?**

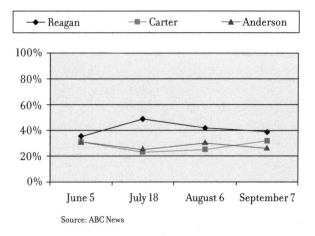

Source: ABC News

There were several reasons why his polling numbers got worse as November loomed. First, he waited until August to choose as his running mate former Wisconsin governor Patrick Lucey, a Democrat. Lucey had limited visibility outside of his home state, so the ticket's name recognition problem remained very serious. People generally only vote for someone they see frequently in the media, and it's difficult to support someone they rarely see on the nightly news, read about in the papers, or see in television commercials.

Second, the press gave him much less attention as the campaign wound down. There's a tendency as an election gets closer for reporters to focus only on those whom political polls deem the top two candidates. Also, Anderson's campaign continued to be consumed with ballot access and organizational problems. Consequently, he never could raise enough money to be competitive.

When Anderson had poll numbers around 20 percent, the League of Women Voters judged his support strong enough to invite him to the first presidential debate. President Carter's handlers were afraid of the additional votes Anderson could gain on a national stage, so they advised Carter not to participate. The president was a no-show, and Anderson debated Reagan. Anderson's slide continued into October, and the League declined to invite him to the lectern for the second debate. This seriously hurt Anderson's ability to get his message and ideas out to the public. That, along with his inability to raise the large sums of money necessary to run a national campaign, sealed his fate. The Federal Election Campaign Act sent millions of dollars in public money to Carter and Reagan; Anderson had to scramble at the last minute for more meager resources to keep his campaign alive.

Consider this: Under federal election laws, Carter and Reagan each received $29 million in public funding, and Anderson $18.5 million. Carter and Reagan each spent about $15 million on television advertising, and Anderson under $2 million. The two major-party candidates each outspent Anderson by more than seven to one, and he still managed to stay competitive in the polls for more than six months.

His run for the White House was truly remarkable, given all the problems he had. Ballot access and campaign organization problems, along with a disinterested media, played into the hands of his opponents.

Anderson's final tally was 6.6 percent, or about 5.7 million votes. Respectable, yes, but disappointing because he could have done so much better. Although Anderson did end up on the ballot in all fifty states and the District of Columbia, his campaign was ultimately underpowered, undermanned, and underfinanced. Had he not taken a trip abroad in July—a "vacation," as some critics put it—he might well have finished higher. Had he been invited to the second debate, it is more than likely that merely being in a three-way contest would have helped buttress his final vote total. And had he not had to focus on raising money just to cope with ballot access issues—money that would have been better spent on TV ads—he would almost certainly have gained still more votes.

As an independent third-party candidate in 1992, H. Ross Perot ran a campaign that was entirely different from John Anderson's. Anderson began as a mainstream Republican who drifted away from the two major political parties; Ross Perot approached the public as a complete outsider.

He was the unlikeliest of presidential hopefuls, at least according to the criteria that most voters traditionally deem important. As mentioned before, he had absolutely no public service experience. His business credentials were impeccable, however. He had been a star salesman at IBM, and he later founded Electronic Data Systems. He successfully competed with IBM and other emerging electronics firms, and eventually became a billionaire.

Perot seized on America's fiscal problems well before Bill

Clinton's famous war room placard—"It's the economy, stupid"—became a Democratic battle cry. What Perot brought to the presidential campaign was a shrewd understanding of the suffering of the middle class during an economic recession. He spoke in simple, commonsense terms and advocated policies like a balanced budget in straightforward words that the American people could easily understand.

The American middle class was being hurt because of unsound fiscal policies, according to Perot, who even skeptics admitted understood business and economics. President Bush was "deep in voodoo," he argued, a reference to the president's criticism of Reagan's original fiscal plan, but one that Bush, soon after he was elected, bought into anyway. Who could ever forget the famous TV clip of Bush at the checkout counter, wondering what a bar code was? It was the starkest indication that the president had no idea what kind of financial difficulties the typical family faced. Bush was out of touch.

Perot's platform was called "United We Stand: How We Can Take Back Our Country." Perot was pro-choice and in favor of strict gun controls, and he strongly supported a balanced budget and the line-item veto. He also suggested that a fifty-cent-a-gallon gas tax would help fill up the nation's treasury and strengthen the spiraling dollar. The Congress had become a slave to deficit spending. Perot looked at this as the single driver of all of our ills.

His campaign took off after he appeared on CNN's *Larry King Live* and 70,000 people phoned his 800 number to encourage him to run. Soon after, a petition drive began, and in two and a half months, Texas volunteers had 250,000 signatures, five times more than the state required to get on the ballot.

Over the next six months, Perot's campaign was chaotically organized—by a largely unpaid staff—but fueled by populist support from almost every corner of the nation.

In a July op-ed in *The Washington Post,* Ed Rollins, Perot's campaign manager, explained the extent of Perot's unwillingness to strategically use his own resources so that the campaign could either broadcast his message or systematically organize his volunteers:

> *More than 5 million volunteers called Perot's 800 number and offered to help. But Perot wouldn't spend any money organizing them, and he wouldn't let his campaign make contact with them. Instead, their names were put on computer cards and stuffed, unused, into a storage closet. . . . He also didn't want to spend his money, even though he had promised me he would pour $150 million into the campaign. Instead, he rejected every budget item, including millions targeted for all-important television advertising. "I'll just go talk to the people on 'Larry King,' " he would tell me.*

Despite his disorganized campaign, in just four months— from February 20 to June 20—Perot went from nearly zero to the lead in the national polls.

In February, Perot scored about 9 percent in preference polls; at the end of April, it was 28 percent; and by June he peaked at 37 percent, ahead of both Bush and Clinton.

Moreover, Perot's support was increasing in core constituencies. Support among women polled went from 19 percent to 26 percent in a month. Among voters under thirty and voters aged thirty to forty-nine, support rose to 32 percent, from 25 and 26 percent, respectively. Regionally, his support jumped in the Sunbelt (9 points, to 37 percent) and even in the South (from 26 to 32 percent).

Figure 12 shows how Perot inexorably moved into the lead by early June 1992, as Figure 11 outlined. It also shows that the bulk of Perot's support seemingly came from Bush—the incumbent president's support level decreased as Perot's vote steadily in-

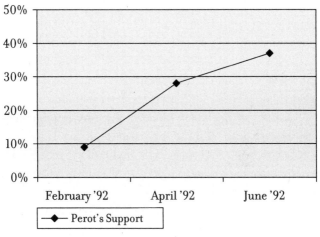

FIGURE 11. If the 1992 Election Were Held Today, Would You Vote for Ross Perot?

Source: Harris, CBS, 1992

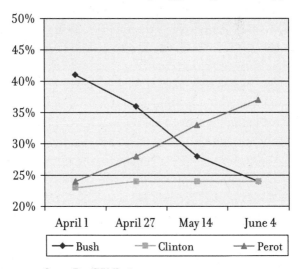

FIGURE 12. Perot's Increasing Support, April–June 1992

Source: *Time*/CNN, Harris

creased. Democrat Bill Clinton saw his support level stay constant, in the low 20s.

In Gallup's June poll, 31 percent of the electorate said that they preferred Perot, and 39 percent felt he could best handle America's economic problems. He was rated strong on leadership qualities (46%) and likability (33.7%), though 74 percent of the registered voters said they "need more information" about what Perot would do if elected. A Harris poll later that same month had Perot leading the incumbent George Bush by four percentage points, 37 to 33, while Bill Clinton trailed with just 25 percent.

By the end of the month, *Political Hotline* had Perot leading in a state-by-state assessment, with 284 electoral votes to 158 for Bush and 16 for Clinton.

The conclusion is clear and obvious. In 1992, there was a candidate with no experience in elected office who was railing about the status quo every day, and six months before the general election, he was clearly the preferred candidate by likely voters.

A successful independent insurgency appeared to be well within reach. Perot initially stuck to his core expertise, the economy, and he insisted that the nation follow a course of fiscal responsibility. In public responses, Perot gave the American public a lesson in Economics 101 by making easy-to-understand points in everyday language. A balanced budget made sense because it was just plain logical. If you have to balance your budget at home, there is no reason the federal government should not have to do the same thing.

Despite the groundswell of support and a growing momentum, Perot began to lose his focus. On July 15, after his name had been placed on the ballot in half the states, he abruptly withdrew from the race. Even after he dropped out, Perot continued touring college campuses as if he were still campaigning and pointedly did not seek to disband his campaign organization. Thus, it was not a complete surprise when he reemerged on October 1, again announcing his official candidacy.

Perot's initial departure from the campaign trail caused a rift among his supporters. Legions of volunteers were bitterly disappointed, but still his book, published during the Republican national convention in Houston, rose to the top of the bestseller list.

On September 16, Perot's camp had obtained the necessary signatures to be on the ballot in all fifty states and the District of Columbia. Two weeks later, Perot announced that he was back in the race and was planning a final five-week-long assault. He spent $37 million that month on half-hour infomercials utilizing his homemade charts and graphs. He was included in all three campaign debates—debates that he may well have won. And even if he did not win those debates, the exposure he received at the very least enhanced his credibility and visibility.

Although he failed to win a single state, Perot finished with 19 percent of the nation's popular vote, the third highest percentage won by a third party in American history (behind Millard Fillmore in 1856 and Theodore Roosevelt in 1912). Third-party advocates can only wonder if that ticket would have received closer to 30 percent or even more had the candidate not behaved so erratically in the last few months before the election.

After Perot failed again in 1996, with his vote slipping to 7 percent in large part because of his exclusion from the fall debates that year, the century's third-party enthusiasm clearly waned. To be sure, Ralph Nader, the Green Party candidate in 2000 and an independent candidate in 2004, who is vehemently opposed to free trade and an ardent environmentalist, became the spokesman for the disenfranchised left, particularly in 2000. Some political pundits believe that he could have been a competitive candidate that year if he had received more visibility from the mainstream media and had been included in the fall debates. And Pat Buchanan, the former Nixon and Reagan aide, and now a TV commentator, emerged as the Reform Party candidate (breaking from the Republicans to represent the far right) and ran in three election cycles, most notably in 2000. But neither Buchanan nor Nader was ever a serious candidate for a frustrated electorate that was abandoning the Republicans and Democrats in droves. Nader and Buchanan had trouble reaching out beyond their very limited constituencies. They were clearly not the kind of third-party candidates who can unite the center of the electorate.

Nader and Buchanan aside, it is very clear that third-party candidacies, however marginalized they have been in the past, have contributed substantially to changing American politics and policy. And it is my contention that regardless of whether an independent actually wins the election, the mere presence of such a candidate on the ballot will invigorate the political debate and almost certainly encourage consensus and conciliation.

A serious independent candidate now can overcome many of the impediments earlier third-party candidates have faced because the nature of the process has changed considerably. I'll explain how in the next chapter.

4

Third-Party Candidates Can Overcome the Impediments

The "ideological divide" separating conservative Republicans and liberal Democrats leaves a vast untended center from which a well-financed independent presidential candidate is likely to emerge in 2008 or, if not then, in 2012.

—ALAN GREENSPAN, former chairman of the Federal Reserve System

ALAN GREENSPAN COULD HAVE BEEN TALKING ABOUT ANY ONE OF A number of people when he made his comment in early 2006. The fact of the matter is that there is a much greater opportunity for a third-party candidate to emerge than most people realize, for a number of ideological and structural reasons.

The political pundits, the Sunday morning talk show commentators, and the party activists from prior campaigns have all got it wrong. Those who have analyzed the recent third-party candidacies as failures—and there have been at least a half-dozen books with extensive postmortems of them—have largely missed the point. The point is that they've had more success and appeal than anyone recognized at the time. The point is not that they lost; it's that they did so miraculously well despite the encumbrances. And if you dig deep into the circumstances of their runs and compare these with the contemporary political culture we have today, you will understand why it could well be different this time around.

The problem for George Wallace, Anderson, and Perot was that the system was stacked against them. Wallace, who basically is perceived as a fringe candidate running on one issue, got close to 14 percent. Anderson, who was not even a factor in the Republican primaries and wasn't even widely known, became very competitive nationally very quickly, and the polls show that if he had been perceived as having a chance to win, he would have done much better. And Perot, who had the thinnest credentials of anyone who ever ran for president, was actually leading the race for almost four months before he dropped out temporarily in July 1992. Even after taking the summer off, Perot proved that a third-party candidate could mount a competitive campaign.

These results show that the American people are hungering for independents or third-party candidates.

All of the problems that were faced by Wallace, Anderson, and Perot—organization, money, ballot access, debate access, media coverage, and the like—can be addressed by the unique political circumstances of 2008. Yes, those three candidates were greatly hampered by the vagaries and impediments of third-party politics, but most of the hurdles they faced can be much more easily overcome now.

To be sure, the Republicans and Democrats have no incentive to change the system, especially now that more and more voters are dissociating themselves from either party. Why would either party rush to support a fairer system of election that could favor their opponent, or a third party? It's never been in their best interests, not then, not now.

But it no longer matters. The dirty little secret of American politics is that things have changed fundamentally.

The impediments of the past are no longer the kinds of stumbling blocks that will necessarily consume a third-party candidate's campaign staff, sap their energy, and force them to focus on problems that can distract them from the main task of running a campaign. Too many changes have occurred and the playing field has been leveled. And even if no third-party candidate appears in 2008, what is happening now has changed politics irrevocably.

Politics has changed dramatically, and we're working with new rules that candidates and their advisers don't fully understand. As a political consultant who has helped to elect a president, I know the landscape. It's no longer as simple as putting a sixty-second political commercial on TV and going to some rallies. The Internet, the continuous news cycle, and the nature of political organizing have changed the way campaigns will be run.

In the past, if you wanted to build an organization, you had to go to the party's power brokers, who might well shut you out. You had to go through their infrastructure (which has a hierarchy and a protocol for step-by-step kingmaking). Obviously this has changed. The old system of working your way up through local politics, paying the required dues and tribute to the Democratic and Republican organizations, has lost its appeal and its importance. We live in a world where a candidacy can be created instantly. Perot, Ventura, Dean, and Ned Lamont, the 2004 Democratic Senate candidate in Connecticut, among others, have proved this.

The primary process is now open to virtually any serious individual who wants to run for president, although challenges such as ballot access for an independent candidate in the general election still exist. But there have been some significant changes in the mood of the electorate that will, under the right circumstances, make getting on the ballot less of a challenge than it has been in the past. We've had a tectonic shift in the mood of the nation—call it the revolt of the middle, or the revenge of the moderates, but what is happening is that there is a huge percentage of voters who are angry at both parties. According to an NBC/*Wall Street Journal* poll in June 2007, Congress had a lower approval rating (23 percent) than the president (whose rating is hovering around 28 percent as I write this). It's a direct response to what the public sees as terminal gridlock. It's much like the emergence of Nixon's silent majority in the 1960s. And these voters will be a major factor in the upcoming election. They are accessible online, they will volunteer, they will contribute, they will file petitions, they will respond, they will participate in a dialogue with the candidates.

And what this says about the campaign process is that there's a new dynamic out there that allows people to communicate not only through TV commercials but also through blogs, e-mail, and interactive websites. They'll be typing late into the night and into the early morning hours, cajoling their peers to get involved, to contribute, to hold meet-ups. They'll look at the alternatives—yes, and they'll find the candidates who speak their language. And they'll go through alternative media, cable TV, satellite TV, late night TV, and talk shows to reach people. And none of this will cost much money.

I can't overstress the word "interactive." There is going to be more pressure for multiple, interactive experiences with the candidates and their campaigns. Call it the chance for "endless debates," some of which will accommodate call-in questions from voters online rather than from a studio audience. This is an area where the voters are actually ahead of the politicians. The voters understand they can have direct access to a campaign; the voters understand they can use the power of blogs; they understand they can have meetings without the candidates. They understand they can contact anyone involved in the campaign at any time they want. It's the politicians and the media that don't yet understand all this.

Take a look at how campaign organizing has changed. In the past, it was very difficult to put together an effective campaign organization. Staffers were far-flung, and there were often petty turf wars and power struggles. This can sap the energy of any campaign. Today, because of modern technology, campaign organizations can reach out to millions of organizers across the nation via the Internet with just a click of the mouse.

You can literally run a campaign with a computer and have an ongoing interactive dialogue that's different from what's happened before, that arguably couldn't exist ten or twelve years ago. You can take the pulse of an election district instantaneously. You can get up to speed on local issues without a huge, expensive advance staff. So it's a new world, a different world.

Take what we saw with Barack Obama, with Ron Paul, with Wesley Clark, with Howard Dean. The people themselves took the initiative in these campaigns by volunteering, by organizing rallies, by getting their neighbors to open their checkbooks. A kind of momentum built up from urban areas throughout the heartlands. It starts in somebody's den on his or her computer, and spreads electronically throughout the neighborhood and then the nation itself. You could almost call it viral campaign organizing.

Look at it from the candidates' point of view: they can do with one click what used to take weeks and months and a lot of money. Direct mail from the finance chairman, while still part of the process, is yesterday's strategy. In many instances, it's inefficient and costly. Now, it's about how people organize on their own, how they find common values. It's about how they use meet-ups, and find each other, and get together as like-minded communities despite the geographical challenges.

And campaigns themselves can be more precise and efficient. A campaign can now organize a state or region; it can funnel efforts and activity where there are electoral votes to be gained. And we still don't know what the potential of this power is. Only a few years ago, if someone had said they were going to announce their candidacy online, we would have laughed. Now it's become de rigueur.

The local political organizations still exist, but they've been

largely marginalized and are almost irrelevant. A new state political organization can morph into existence in ways that nobody
could have predicted. Who would have thought that there would be
tens of thousands of volunteers who could instantly respond, meet
online or in person, and correspond through blogs and also
through social-networking sites like MySpace and Facebook? The
concept of what a political organization is and can do has changed.
It is so different from what existed before, and it is evolving so
quickly that the politicians don't really know what its capacity is.
The online community is still a largely untapped force.

A nontraditional candidate who needs to gain ballot access
will eventually be able to unleash this force. Too many third-
party or independent candidates have had trouble getting on the
ballots in key states because the system was stacked against
them. Their campaign organizations had to waste precious time
and money gathering the number of signatures required to get
on each state's ballot. Now, teams of volunteers can easily be mobilized to gather these signatures quickly and less painfully than
ever before.

The main requirements for an independent candidate to gain
ballot access are as follows:

First, he or she will need approximately 800,000 signatures
to gain ballot access in fifty states and Washington, D.C. Every
state, of course, has different requirements. Louisiana doesn't
require any signature petition, and Tennessee requires only 25
signatures. In California you have to get 158,371 signatures. In
Texas, a candidate not only needs 74,108 signatures from voters
who did not already vote in the 2008 presidential primaries, but
they must also be gathered in a specific ninety-day period in early
2008 or they're invalid.

In addition, the candidate must be a registered independent
to get on the ballot as an independent candidate (as opposed to a
third-party candidate). Nine states require a person to be a regis-

tered independent in order to run as an independent presidential candidate.

But a smart campaign organization can now enlist supporters to do a lot of the organizing necessary for ballot access in difficult states using the Internet, making the whole process itself more manageable.

Look for the debate process to change dramatically in the upcoming election as well. The conventional wisdom of past cycles no longer applies. To assume that the old static model of campaigns and traditional debates will continue to exist is wrong. To not look beyond the conventional model is ultimately a myopic defense of the system, witting or unwitting.

In the past, the Republican and Democratic presidential candidates have faced off in a series of three televised evening sessions, usually a few weeks before election day. This format is somewhere between insulting and silly. *Washington Post* columnist David Ignatius wrote, "What we have are not so much debates as the kind of inane interviews given by contestants in Miss America pageants. Republicans and Democrats speak to their respective bases, rather than to the nation; most candidates stay within the boundaries of what's deemed to be safe."

We've already seen a lineup of candidates from the major parties in preprimary debates—certainly any dialogue is better than nothing. But these have largely amounted to free-for-alls where each candidate presents a prepackaged spiel after being asked a question by the moderator. These are not debates in any traditional sense of the word—as you know if you've ever been on a high school or college debating team, or even watched a real debate. They are for the most part carefully crafted campaign scripts delivered by the candidates. This is frequently insulting to the intelligence of any American interested in really learning what each candidate has to offer the country. When are the candidates going to get it? We understand the scheme. We rarely get to see the give-

and-take that would reveal how a presidential aspirant might truly think on his or her feet and respond under real pressure.

As will be shown in chapter 8, there are already pressures to change the nature and format of presidential debates during the 2008 campaign. Concepts like the YouTube debates on CNN and the "mashup," or online dialogue between the candidates, sponsored by Yahoo! News and the Huffington Post underscore the increasing importance of interactivity in the process—a trend in the nature of debates and political communications that will almost certainly continue should a third-party candidate enter the race.

Now, let's talk about money, a crucial part of the political game. Here's the conventional wisdom about money and third-party candidates: Every presidential campaign cycle, it costs more money to get into the game. Most independent campaigns suffer because they can't raise enough money to get adequate name recognition for a candidate and thus mount a strong showing. If you're wealthy, you can do it yourself, as Jon Corzine proved in New Jersey and Michael Bloomberg has successfully illustrated twice in New York City.

But the fundraising game has changed. You don't necessarily have to be a billionaire to run. You can become known without money, and you can raise money without being known nationally. It's still an extremely expensive proposition to get elected president, but the donation pool and possibilities have grown exponentially, thanks to e-mail, inexpensive solicitations, and low-cost fundraising infrastructure. In the past, you had a finance chairman, and he set up regional offices, and there were others in the food chain who organized cocktail parties and dinners where fat cats were the norm. The quid pro quo of these events was self-evident. Give a large campaign contribution, and you expected access to the candidate; it's a form of soft-core lobbying.

This is no longer the only way to do it. Howard Dean, Barack Obama, and even Ron Paul have proved that you can fill the campaign coffers with small contributions if you use the Internet to solicit donations. Check the box with your mouse and enter your credit card number. You can set up a network where you can ask for two- and three-figure checks—and the people who send them do not expect to knock on the White House door asking to sleep in the Lincoln Bedroom if you win. They're merely grateful to support someone with sensible, populist values that mirror their own. Again, the game has changed.

The expansion of the media, the growth of the Internet, and the continuous news cycle make it easier than ever for an independent candidate to gain traction in a race. Before cable TV and computer networking, third-party candidates had to rely on political-beat reporters and network news commentators to cover them. They rarely received the coverage they deserved. A generation ago, there were only a few outlets for national political news on television. Today, there are nine major networks that regularly gather and dispense political news. They are ABC, CBS, NBC, Fox, CNN, MSNBC, Fox News, PBS, and NPR. These networks have a huge amount of airtime to fill. We are inundated with every step and misstep every candidate takes, early and often. With the World Wide Web and expanded cable and satellite TV coverage, it's less likely that an insurgent's candidacy will be underreported or overlooked by mainstream media.

In March 2007, more than five hundred people attended a two-day conference on online politics at George Washington University in Washington, D.C. The attendees included political consultants, campaign operatives, and start-up Internet company representatives, and they discussed how the Internet was going to figure in the 2008 race. It's clear that the wonks are climbing on board, and they're desperate to understand and utilize the power of the Internet.

"Decentralization" is one of the key words that you'll hear more of in cyber-campaigning. It was used by the Dean campaign group, led by Joe Trippi, that was nestled in Vermont creating Dean's insurgent campaign in 2003–2004. It was the Dean philosophy that campaign headquarters had to be distributed throughout the nation, and that the candidate didn't really "control" the flow of information; rather, the people did. This was a fundamental change in how campaigns are run. For one of the first times ever, it was the campaign volunteers and not the candidate and his staff who were the leading edge of the effort.

Today, as we approach the 2008 election, the traditional impediments to mounting an independent campaign are much more easily surmountable than in the past.

This is a unique time in our history because these changes are coupled with a revolt of the moderates. Fundamentally, what the people are looking for is someone who offers commonsense solutions, no matter what party they represent. Will it be an independent or third-party candidate whom voters respond to? Or perhaps one of the candidates already running will recognize this and offer a nonpartisan appeal to these voters.

The voters have become wiser, and they have more tools at their disposal to make a discerning decision about a candidate. They have decided to, at least at first, look elsewhere, as a new modern era of third-party and serious independent candidates has emerged. The political experts did hundreds of focus groups, and they discovered something that most of us intuitively understand every fall: people have traditionally had significant doubt about both major-party candidates and their parties in most races. Many have become used to holding their noses and voting for the least objectionable candidate. Now, they are unhappy with the incumbent president, and they're equally unhappy with their senators and representatives.

In short, the voters are desperate for change, and now they have the tools to take matters into their own hands and begin to effect that change themselves.

5

The Internet and 24-Hour News

*I've been in politics for forty years, and these days everything
I've learned about politics is totally irrelevant because
there's this uncontrollable thing called the Internet.
Washington insiders don't know what to make of it.*

—ED ROLLINS, former Perot campaign manager
and Reagan administration official

HOW IS POLITICS DIFFERENT TODAY FROM A GENERATION AGO? AND
why? Some things certainly haven't changed: many of the challenges we face today are the same ones we've faced in the past. But the circumstances are different now. We have 24-hour news cycles and high-speed communication links that connect potential voters with organizers, and that allow candidates to emerge instantaneously. Ross Perot emerged instantaneously because of an 800 number. Wesley Clark emerged instantaneously in 2004; Ned Lamont, in the 2004 Connecticut Senate Democratic primary against Senator Joe Lieberman. Their emergence into the public eye was facilitated by a continuous news flow and new communications tools. Senator Fred Thompson's name was floated as a presidential possibility almost continually because of this constant, unceasing news cycle. Thompson got ten points in

the polls even before he decided to run. After he announced his candidacy, it is not surprising that he more than doubled his support, moving into at least second place in Republican trial heats—in large part because of strategically placed postings on the Web by his supporters and effective use of cable news. Even Republican fringe candidates on the right, like libertarian Ron Paul, have seen their support base and their funding sources grow exponentially because of the relatively new communication tools.

What is my point here? *A previously unknown candidate can break through today without spending a lot of money.* In 2004 Howard Dean reached critical mass by using the Internet. The Net enabled him to overcome the daunting challenge of making himself known during the early phases of the campaign. But this relatively new technology can do much more. It's a tool for social networking, organizing, and fundraising among the masses. The Web 2.0—the generation of user-friendliness—has ushered in sites that emphasize user-generated content, social networking, and interactive sharing. Twenty-first-century technology offers a new form of democracy within our political structure.

Had Ross Perot been a candidate today—and I'm hypothesizing very conservatively—his campaign would have been an even greater media event than it was fifteen years ago, and he would have generated even more initial enthusiasm than he ultimately did. The blogs alone would have greatly helped his cause, and the tools available now would have allowed him to build a full-blown campaign organization virtually overnight.

Here is a brief summary of how technology has changed the political game, and how all of these offshoots on the World Wide Web will aid a third-party candidate:

- **SOCIAL NETWORKING.** YouTube, Meetup, MySpace, and Facebook, as well as various politically oriented sites, have localized political organizing and campaign events. People of like minds find one another instantaneously online; there's no need for expensive direct mailings and phone banks to rally supporters.

- **INTERACTIVE WEBSITES.** Candidates can now communicate directly with voters without the filter of the media. They can post increasingly specific information online about their positions and campaign themselves, and target their communications to any immediate concerns that might emerge. Candidates can also get direct, unfettered, rapid feedback about the issues that concern voters most. The result will be that candidates can be more responsive to the electorate and maintain interactive dialogue with voters.

- **SPECIALIZED WEBSITES.** Candidates can develop focused websites to do rapid response to attacks or to raise money at particularly opportune times. For example, in November 2007, Hillary Clinton started a website, the Fact Hub, to enable her to offer instantaneous rebuttal to attacks that might be leveled against her candidacy. The subjects of the attacks might range from serious issues, like immigration, to more trivial issues, like whether or not she actually left a tip in a restaurant.* The fact of the matter is, in the current environment, everything—no matter how unimportant—is a potential issue in campaign 2008. Ron Paul's campaign set up a website, thisnovember5th.com, to try to rally antiestablishment sentiment on Guy Fawkes' Day. The initiative was a huge success, raising over $4 million, a one-day record for online fundraising.

---

*A waitress in an Iowa restaurant said in response to a reporter's questions about Clinton's tipping habits: "You people are really nuts. There are kids dying in the war, the price of oil is high. There are better things in the world to think about than who served Hillary Clinton at Maid-Rite, and who received a tip and who did not."

- **BLOGGING.** Anyone with an opinion and a passion to distribute their views can have a daily or weekly blog. The Net has spawned a nation of quasi-journalists. They include thoughtful commentators inspired by Thomas Paine, intense partisans who are offshoots of Matt Drudge, and everything in between. The video blog is the newest iteration of this kind of communication.

- **SEARCH ENGINE OPTIMIZATION.** What used to be called "push technology" has now evolved into a sophisticated advertising play. Candidates can pay to get their messages listed on the first screen as certain keywords are typed into search engines like Yahoo, Google, Northern Lights, and Ask.com. The number of "eyeballs"—as they are known in the trade—reached per dollar is remarkably large. When you type in a candidate's name or an issue, ads you may be interested in will go to the top of the queue.

- **INSTANT VIDEO.** Speeches, rallies, and important messages can be videotaped by the campaign and immediately put online to reach millions of viewers.

- **TEXT MESSAGING.** Campaigns can gather phone lists of active supporters simply by asking people to send in a text message code and "join" the candidate's team. Instant communication with thousands and thousands of supporters then becomes immediately possible.

All these items add up to one incontrovertible conclusion: We'll have access to campaign news all the time. You'll know more than you ever did before about any potential candidate, and you'll know it sooner and in greater detail.

The technology of picture cellphones, portable access to e-mail, and TV devoted to news all day long is just beginning to have an effect on the political front. We really don't know to what extent this intersection of Internet, cable and satellite TV, and instant news will affect campaigns to come. A single YouTube ad can galvanize America—or cause a front-runner to stumble. Although some candidates have wholly or partly unveiled their candidacies online, like Hillary Clinton and Fred Thompson, it's clear that nobody has figured out how to unleash the seemingly unlimited potential and power of the Web on a single presidential campaign. All the pundits, the consultants, and the political pollsters are still learning the rules of the game and what it is possible to achieve.

Let's just take a look at the cellphone, a ubiquitous piece of technology among young and old. With 75 percent of Americans owning cellphones, this could prove to be a crucial form of communication between candidate and voter. As I write this, the campaigns of Barack Obama, Hillary Clinton, and John Edwards have all embraced these devices as campaign tools.

Aides for Obama said they'll use text messaging to organize events and urge supporters to donate money. Hours before a Democratic forum at Howard University in the summer of 2007, his campaign sent this message: "Debate tonight! Watch Barack Obama. . . ."

"Your cell phone is probably the one piece of technology that is with you all the time," Joe Rospars, Obama's director of new media, told *The Washington Post.* Rospars is responsible for his candidate's "mobile" campaign, which began in June 2007. He added, "The reality is, I don't think there's a campaign or a political organization right now that has figured out how to smartly use this technology. There's going to be a lot of experimentation."

Rospars makes a salient point, and it's one I constantly convey. We don't yet know how much power can be unleashed by today's technology in a presidential campaign. The rules have changed, and yet nobody is quite certain what these new rules are.

I suspect we're going to find out.

It just hasn't happened yet, but we're poised to see an independent going outside the system to seize these powerful opportunities and ride them to the top of the polls.

In addition, computer networking has altered the campaign landscape.

In 1993, after Perot made his run for the Oval Office, only 22 percent of U.S. households had a home computer. Many people had no idea what "online" meant. E-mail had not yet become an essential part of our lives. Today, there are more than 240 million home computers among 300 million people. Two surveys put the percentage of online households that subscribe to a high-speed broadband service at 42 and 48 percent. Among Internet users, U.S. broadband penetration exceeded 70 percent for the first time in April 2006. Most of us use the Internet and are wired for speed, making political communication easier and more effective.

If you want to see a startling example of how much the Internet is going to affect the 2008 election, you need not go further than Phil de Vellis's video commercial for Barack Obama. In early 2007, it was all over the Internet, viewable on YouTube. It's a take-off of the famous "1984" spot that Apple did for the Super Bowl that year, in which it depicted its competition—ostensibly IBM—as a company of lemmings, marching in lockstep off a cliff. In de Vellis's ad, however, you see the face of Hillary Clinton on a jumbo screen, and she's heard hoping we'll solve our problems by starting a conversation and talking about the issues openly and honestly. In the aisle between the seated lemmings is a lithe blonde athlete flinging a sledgehammer into the screen, where it hits Hillary in the face and explodes.

Shocking? Perhaps. Whether it was an effective ad or not can be endlessly debated. But what is not in dispute was that the ad generated enormous attention when it was posted on YouTube—more attention than much of what was going on in the various campaigns at that time. Similarly, when Hillary Clinton posted her own ad online in June 2007, mocking *The Sopranos,* it won her substantial critical acclaim, helped soften her image, and similarly dominated the campaign news for a few days. The guy who produced the Obama ad did have a tangential connection to the Obama campaign, but he posted the spot on YouTube as an individual. He likes Barack and does not like Hillary, and while he did have some links to a company that had already done some work for Obama, the point is that *anyone could have done it.* And by using stock footage, any voter can create a single ad for next to nothing.

Welcome to the new electronic world of electoral politics, where firestorms are just waiting to start and spread. And yes, the 2008 election will be different from the 2004 election—and even the 2006 midterm election. Generations of people who knew nothing of YouTube, social networking, and blogging four years ago now use the Internet for virtually all facets of day-to-day life: getting the news, shopping, and socializing.

Even the news cycle has become more condensed since the last election. The large Web organizations have hired specialists and executives to develop political sites on the Internet and to pitch candidates who want to buy their services in cyberspace. Brick-and-mortar news outlets, print, and network and cable TV all update their sites with breaking news in a matter of minutes.

The Internet is changing politics in a way that we are just beginning to understand. The Web has leveled the playing field for candidates who begin their efforts without vast resources, and changed the way campaigns are run. Now we have search engines, news websites, campaign home pages, podcasts, and no dearth of blogs.

Anyone with an Internet connection and a little pluck can become an instant pundit, or at least influence the speed (and often the slant) with which a news story develops. It's difficult to overestimate how much this could affect a presidential campaign. The expansion of public discourse hasn't had this much exciting potential since the telegraph first revolutionized communication. (Western Union, by the way, sent its last telegram in 2006.) We can take the pulse of any contest, analyze a demographic, decipher a psychographic, and deconstruct an election district in astonishing detail. These methods have become powerful tools for campaign managers, pollsters, and strategists, who can determine the probable outcome in any given zip code. Not only do we know where you live, we know—with some degree of accuracy—who you're likely to vote for on November 4, 2008.

Technology shifts began to rapidly alter the pace of presidential campaigns when Ross Perot ran as a third-party candidate. *Newsweek*'s Howard Fineman called it "talk show democracy." Perot's legion of volunteers relied on an electronic web of "interactive" television and radio shows, 800 numbers, phone banks, fax machines, and computer billboards. Perot's first infomercial aired on CBS and tallied 16 million viewers, and according to the Nielsen ratings, it beat out *Quantum Leap* on NBC and *Full House* on ABC.

Perot cleverly engaged voters by asking them to respond to his ideas and proposals with phone calls and faxes. It had a positive effect. It was the first advance in interactive communication between candidate and voter since the whistle-stop train campaigns of the past. "Voters and leaders are sick of mediating institutions, of go-betweens," said political scientist Christopher Arterton, co-author of *The Electronic Commonwealth.* "They want direct communication." Perot was one of the first candidates to take advantage of the technique of using lengthy, unfiltered "messages," rather than straightforward thirty- or sixty-second spots.

It took a gubernatorial race, however, to first test the modern communications movement. In 1998, Jesse Ventura, best known in a prior life as a professional wrestler, was elected Minnesota governor as the Reform Party candidate in an upset that left many a political pundit reeling. Ventura used the Internet as a tool for mobilizing volunteers and voters, and while it's impossible to measure its impact precisely, it's clear that his own campaign organizers believed that he could not have won the statehouse without it.

In addition to maintaining a Ventura website that featured daily photos and updates, the Reform Party candidate's campaign relied heavily on e-mail to organize thousands of volunteers throughout the state. Early on, Ventura bought into the idea that the Net could make a difference in his low-budget bid for office. Cynics could say he had no choice because his opponents had much deeper pockets. Ventura's Republican and Democratic opponents each outspent him five to one. Ventura had only one paid staffer throughout the campaign.

"It's tailor-made for my campaign," Ventura said of the Internet several months before his victory. "It's reaching a huge amount of people at a very low price." The director of his website, Phil Madsen, said, "The Internet for us served as the nervous system for the campaign. The web site was not the difference; it was the mobilization."

That is probably an accurate assessment. The Ventura campaign used the Internet primarily as a behind-the-scenes coordinating tool. The campaign's final push, a seventy-two-hour caravan drive throughout Minnesota, was organized and coordinated entirely by e-mail and through the campaign's website. Madsen sent out an e-mail to his 3,000-member list, called Jesse Net, inviting volunteers to a meeting. More than 250 people attended. Organizing the meeting took less than a day and a half.

Ventura won by three percentage points over Norm Coleman, the Republican mayor of St. Paul. Hubert H. Humphrey III, the Democratic candidate, finished third. Madsen concluded, "It proves that democracy can still work in America. It doesn't have to be about money and it doesn't have to be about career politicians."

The whole issue of instant communication via the World Wide Web became an integral part of the Gore-Bush race in 2000. Who could forget the comment attributed to Gore that he "invented" the Internet? (Even if he didn't really say it.) It was indeed unfortunate for his supporters, because Gore likely was the most technologically advanced candidate in presidential politics to date: he actually used a laptop rather than relying on aides to print out and send his e-mail.

In 2003, it was the Democratic hopeful, Howard Dean, who took a page out of Ventura's playbook to jump-start an underfinanced campaign. His early supporters were known affectionately as "Deaniacs," and many of those who voted for him during the primaries discovered him on the Internet.

When Joe Trippi signed on to manage Howard Dean's presidential campaign in early 2003, the campaign had only $100,000, a staff of seven, and 432 known supporters. The conventional wisdom was that Dean, a medical doctor (he kept up his practice even as a public servant) and little-known Vermont governor, would be lucky to survive the New Hampshire primary. Trippi imagined he would be working for three months and then going home.

In nine months, by the time of the Iowa caucus on January 19, 2004, Dean became the front-runner for the Democratic nomination, and his campaign had amassed close to $50 million— including a record-setting $15.8 million in the fourth quarter of 2003, mostly from ordinary Americans giving $100 or less. Trippi wrote in his Dean Nation blog that "never—until now—would there have been any hope of one million Americans contributing $100 each to take back their country and promote a common vision for the future of the nation. Maybe it will be two million who contribute $50. But the Internet makes that possible. . . . The tools, the energy, the leadership, and the right candidate . . . are all in place."

Clearly, American voters were making a statement about the status quo, and the Internet was the most convenient medium in which to do it. Dean was the only candidate who unabashedly opposed the invasion of Iraq, which stimulated the bulk of his early support. And the "wired generation" was the first to connect with his positions on issues like jobs, health care, and education.

The surge of Internet use in this time period played the critical role in Dean's breakthrough. It began with a few hundred Dean organizers communicating among themselves on social-networking sites, and spread to colorful Internet and e-mail fundraising appeals on the Dean for America website. Eventually, the attack strategy of an army of bloggers propelled him to national prominence.

How the Web helped Dean reach critical mass makes an instructional story of modern campaigning. In the spring of 2003, the liberal blog MyDD.com posted a news item saying that the first Dean supporters in cities across the country were using Meetup.com—a Web-based social-networking site—to locate other Dean supporters in their communities.

Like Ventura five or six years earlier, the Dean campaign didn't initially have the resources to pay for a large field staff. Those close to the campaign saw Meetup as an attractive replacement for its costly alternatives, an ideal forum for locating and gathering highly motivated campaign volunteers, nurturing their enthusiasm, and ensuring large turnouts at Dean campaign events. Throughout the campaign, Meetup members were on hand for letter-writing campaigns, get-out-the-vote initiatives, and whatever else was on the staff's agenda. The Dean technology team also developed a piece of software called GetLocal, which anyone with a computer could download, then enter a zip code and find the nearest rally or meeting. DeanLink followed, the campaign's version of Friendster, a site that allowed people with similar interests to get together online.

Clearly, the self-expression generated by blogs—which frequently are nothing more than online diaries by people who have a lot of free time to write (usually as unpaid authors)—promulgated the maverick image of the candidate that might not have shown through conventional media coverage. The Dean campaign created the first blog for a political candidate and named it Call to Action.

Dean himself saw the value of the Internet in spreading his message quickly across America. Outside of a "meet-up" (usually meet-ups were mini campaign rallies, often held in a Starbucks), Dean said, "More than four thousand Dean supporters have been to a meet-up nationwide. You see, we are bringing people together. Viral marketing works." In assessing the impact his technology had on his campaign strategy, Dean said, "The Internet community is wondering what its place in the world of politics is. Along comes this campaign to take back the country for ordinary human beings, and the best way you can do that is through the Net. We listen. We pay attention. If I give a speech and the blog people don't like it, next time I change the speech."

Dean's comment does underscore one of the problems with the Web and the way liberal bloggers have used it. Politicians, significantly more on the left than the right, have become inordinately sensitive to the impact of the blogosphere, so much so that the Democratic Party and particularly its primary candidates have been pushed disproportionately to the left or have distracted others from the main issues facing the country.*

Howard Dean faced that challenge during his presidential campaign and encountered an arguably more serious challenge—a challenge that doomed his candidacy.

---

*In September 2007, a congressional debate over General Petraeus's progress report on the war in Iraq was largely derailed by controversy over a MoveOn.org ad mocking him and questioning his patriotism. The Democrats lost a key opportunity and attention turned from our failures in Iraq to a quasi-offensive and inappropriate ad.

Dean's campaign ultimately fizzled after one widely remembered moment. He shrieked with enthusiasm during a speech after a third-place finish in the Iowa caucus—all because he was responding to a crowd that was shouting its pledge of support. "Dean Loses Steam After Scream" was the operative headline. It was called the "I Have a Scream" speech as well. His favorable news coverage dropped from 58 percent prior to Iowa to only 39 percent in the week between the Iowa and New Hampshire primaries.

The speech itself may not have been so damaging. It was the repetition of the short segment both on television and on the Web that led voters to view him as unpresidential. His charisma quotient precipitously dropped in a single fifteen-second moment. It was as if he went from charmer to hyena. Cable channels kept replaying the scream. By the time media trackers reported that the clip had aired at least *seven hundred times,* campaign manager Trippi complained that the way the networks were using it was "unfair . . . it was entertainment masquerading as news."

It can certainly be argued that modern political campaigns on the state and local level could not be waged without the Internet. In fact, technology has had a profound effect on the outcomes of several gubernatorial and congressional races.

In Texas in 2006, the Internet helped drive support for two independent candidates for governor, Carole Keeton "Grandma" Strayhorn, a former state comptroller, and Richard "Kinky" Friedman, a country and western singer with no previous political experience. Neither of the two was particularly technologically sophisticated, but their combined 30 percent of the vote in that election demonstrated the power of alternative means of communication like the Internet in attracting visibility and building support for third-party candidates who are given little chance to win significant mainstream support.

The Internet's influence was felt in a number of campaigns in the 2006 midterm congressional election. In Senate campaigns in Missouri and Montana, voters were flooding the electronic airwaves with blogs in the last midterm election. In addition, House Democratic candidates Paul Hodes in New Hampshire and Joe Sestak in Pennsylvania owed their early support to a set of liberal bloggers who championed their cause. Both won on election day.

In Montana, as noted above, bloggers championed an unknown Democratic Senate candidate, Jon Tester. Similarly, these electronic diarists helped Jim Webb gather ten thousand signatures in three weeks to get on the Democratic primary ballot and take on the Republican incumbent George Allen in the Virginia Senate race. Allen himself saw his campaign implode because of an alleged racist slur that was initially captured by a handheld video camera, and was subsequently broadcast widely across the Internet. Those two Democratic victories were critical in tipping the balance of the Senate, and the Internet was critical to their success.

Perhaps most significantly, Connecticut bloggers waged a daily assault on Democratic senator Joe Lieberman, while lavishing positive attention on his anti–Iraq War primary challenger, Ned Lamont. A newcomer to politics, Lamont was virtually unknown when he began his campaign, and his victory in the Democratic primary over one of Washington's best-known senators is a clear testament to the power of bloggers. The Lamont campaign website linked to seventeen friendly blogs, while his consultants kept up almost daily contact with as many as 150 bloggers.

When Lamont upset Lieberman in the primary, the "Netroots" movement, as it was called by *Time* magazine, had finally made a definitive difference on the political stage. (In the general election, Lamont lost to Lieberman, who ran as an independent.) The much-hyped Internet activists of the Howard Dean presidential campaign, liberal blogs like Daily Kos, and activist groups like MoveOn.org (compulsively pro-Democrat) had generated lots of buzz, but few results at the ballot box until Lamont defeated Lieberman—one of the great upsets in American political history.

Political analysts argued that in a way Lieberman defeated himself because of his staunch support of the war in Iraq. This was partly true, no doubt. But Lamont built significant early support through the Web and particularly the blogger community. The limits of the Web as an organizing tool were also clearly seen in the Lamont campaign. Although he won the primary, he and his supporters were never able to broaden his support, whether online or offline, to appeal to enough Connecticut voters to overcome Senator Lieberman's campaign as an independent. Indeed, the power of a centrist, nonpartisan campaign was evident in the general election when Lieberman transformed himself from a Democrat into a consensus-seeking independent who only wanted to do what was best for Connecticut, regardless of politics.

So while the Internet is hardly a panacea, I think we'll see plenty of surprises in future elections thanks to the communications advances that have been made in the last few years.

I may sound a bit utopian about all of this, but it many ways, the people now own their own printing presses. In the last two or three years, blog fever has escalated to epidemic status. Today, it is the essence of cyber-gossip, and anyone's and everyone's opinion can easily be updated, posted, and spread all over the globe in minutes and at any hour. There will be more Matt Drudges sifting through the fine print and circulating what they find out in minutes and hours, not days. These weblogs have proved that, to a very large degree, we're a nation with an active subculture of compulsive bloviators; it's like one continuous cocktail party attended by millions. For the rest of this year, the all-consuming dinner conversation topic will be "Who do you think will win in November?"

Meanwhile, it's useful to ponder the following question: Has the Internet replaced network news and local newspapers as the place we look for our regular dose of news? "Replace" may be too strong a verb at this point, but the Internet probably is the main reason that newspaper readership has been declining. "During the 2006 midterms, twice as many Americans said they used the

Internet as their main source of political news and information than did in the last midterm election," according to Lee Rainie, the director of the nonpartisan Pew Internet & American Life Project in Washington, D.C. Rainie found that 31 percent of Americans used the Internet during the 2006 campaign to discuss the various races through e-mail and get political information. In a January 2007 Pew survey, one in four Americans said they went to the Internet for election information.

Those in power at the biggest technology companies, namely Yahoo and Google, have taken note, and they are in the process of forging alliances with the political campaigns.

Yahoo already has a director of election strategy, and his job description includes providing news feeds and customized home pages about the election issues to Web surfers. The ultimate goal is to connect candidates with potential voters. This is in addition to the portal's already popular services, which connect people via e-mail and message boards, to debate the election campaign on computer screens. So far, more than seven hundred groups have been formed for those who want to discuss "Decision '08." Yahoo also recently introduced a YouTube-like service called "You Witness News," which allows the site's devotees to upload their own video clips from events around the country.

If Yahoo is involved in the upcoming election, you can correctly speculate that Google, the nation's ubiquitous search engine, will be speeding alongside in lockstep. Google is aggressively promoting various campaign services—Google ads, Google analysis, YouTube, and others—that it hopes campaign strategists will find effective. You can be certain that more than a few campaign ad directors will be buying Google space to target their online videos to specific regions and states. The site will allow them to track site visits ("eyeballs") and precisely aim future initiatives so they will reach potential supporters and voters.

In an effort to generate buzz for its site, not to mention bring in some business, Google has invited the major candidates to its headquarters in Mountain View, California, for a meet-and-greet lunch.

YouTube's presence already can be felt with its YouChoose '08, a page that in the spring of 2007 already listed videos of twelve major presidential candidates. At this writing, Mitt Romney was leading the pack with sixty-five videos posted, and he was followed by John McCain (thirty-three), Joe Biden (thirty-one), and John Edwards (twenty-seven). YouTube, of course, has a news and politics editor, and the site has a politics-specific video blog called CitizenTube.

MySpace, naturally, could not stand still. In perhaps the most closely watched Internet move in 2007, the Web's largest social-networking site introduced a section on politics aimed particularly at those who are following the presidential race. Known as the Impact Channel, it's an online version of a town kiosk. Campaign strategists will pay close attention to the impact it has on young voters—the site is aimed at people in their twenties who don't leave home without the latest in electronic accoutrements. Some 86 percent of the American users of MySpace are of voting age. And that doesn't count the number of seventeen-year-olds who will be eligible to vote in the next election. Tom Anderson, one of the site's founders, told *The New York Times,* "MySpace has a method of reaching people who are historically not interested in voting. . . . In the same way they learn about their friends, they could learn about a candidate." Will this increase voter turnout? It almost certainly will.

Anderson went on to say that the Impact Channel will also feature voter registration tools that could be a virtual response to the "Rock the Vote" initiatives at concerts used in past elections. And, of course, MySpace users will be able to make campaign contributions via the site. So far, the campaigns of Barack Obama,

Hillary Clinton, Rudy Giuliani, Mitt Romney, John Edwards, Joe Biden, and Dennis Kucinich have launched official pages on the MySpace site.

Chris Hughes, one of the founders of the networking site Facebook, went on leave to work for the Obama campaign full-time. Facebook is the networking version of the freshman year-books that were must-reading for college students in the prehistoric era of technology. Recently, Facebook opened its site to anyone with a computer. It's now a social-networking site that is open to all, not only to college students. Imagine the impact it will have on the 2008 presidential election.

As candidates and voters grow more comfortable with this new technology, the Internet will move from serving as an adjunct to traditional campaign techniques to replacing them. Expensive campaign methods relied on by strategists in the past seem perhaps somewhat less important in today's elections: phone banks making automated calls, fundraisers, and direct mail will now co-exist with lower-cost alternatives like e-mail lists, interactive websites, candidate and volunteer blogs, and text messaging via BlackBerrys and cellphones. These initiatives will continue to revolutionize the science of political campaigning as political consultants catch up with the technology and become more sophisticated themselves.

Think of it: A candidate can send out millions of e-mail solicitations to interested parties for a fraction of the price of a direct mail campaign—and have them land on the screens of cellphones and PDAs where the audience is captive and willing to read the messages. In a campaign I worked on in Korea in 2002, the winning candidate used text messaging to augment his voter turnout efforts among younger voters after early exit polls showed turnout lagging in this key voter segment. These efforts may well have made the difference between victory and defeat in that election, and we can envision something similar happening here in campaign 2008 as well.

The presidential election in 2008 will be unlike any other in our nation's history. Why? Because in October the candidates will be unleashing a torrent of political commercials on the screens of our cellphones as we commute to work in the morning. That's never happened before. In 2008, we will see more candidates broadcasting their message via podcasts. Social-networking websites like Friendster and Facebook can rapidly transmit the latest campaign statements and ads to our cellphone screens.

Uninterrupted 24-hour news means that any tidbit of news can now be transmitted instantly and analyzed at once. The new technology is minting new political wonks, new junkies, and involved voters by the hundreds of thousands in election districts across the nation.

The television age in politics isn't over, not by a long shot. But the Internet, with all its interactive potential, has begun to take its own place among mainstream communication techniques.

Every candidate now understands the importance of viral marketing using the new technology. Traditional impediments to a successful third-party candidacy, such as the need to develop a campaign organization and mobilize volunteers to secure ballot access are now far less onerous than they've been before. If you have a thin campaign chest, the bloggers can help fill it up. And they can collect those required ballot signatures in a flash.

Perhaps most important, the fast news cycle and the Internet will make it more likely to accommodate issues raised by third-party candidates, especially those that are avoided or glossed over by the major-party candidates. Moreover, the Web can also help a third-party candidate mobilize disaffected centrists who may not blog and may not be traditional political activists, but are very interested in politics and are also Web-savvy. A study by the E-Voter Institute, for example, has found that heavy online consumers of political information, liberals and conservatives alike, frequently e-mail friends and families about a candidate, contribute, and attend events in response to what they see online. Indeed, the study concluded that political consultants consistently underestimated the impact of the Internet's tools for reaching voters, who are increasingly likely to seek information online and want candidates of all types to campaign online.

In the past, it has been the left that has been most sophisticated and effective in using the Web. But as campaign 2008 unfolds, there is every reason to believe that disaffected voters in the center can be mobilized through the use of this new, increasingly vital technology in organizing an insurgent campaign and building a new national organization of a type never really seen or built before. ·

6

How Campaign Organizing Has Changed

[The Internet] is a very disruptive technology. And it is going to be very destabilizing to the political establishment of both parties. Somebody could come along and raise $200 million and have 600,000 people on the streets working for them without any party structure in the blink of an eye.

—Joe Trippi, senior adviser for the 2008 John Edwards campaign

IT'S FEBRUARY 20, 1992, AND ROSS PEROT IS ON *LARRY KING LIVE,* INSISTing that he's not going to run for president. But King begins to press him gently. Here is the key exchange between the two:

> KING: Can you give me a scenario in which you'd say, OK, I'm in?
> PEROT: Number one, I will not run as either a Democrat or Republican, because I will not sell out to anybody, but to the American people, and I will sell out to them.
> KING: So you'd run as an independent?
> PEROT: Number two, if you're that serious, you register me in 50 states . . .

If that happened, Perot continued, he'd then spend $50 million to $100 million to get elected. In retrospect, the interview seems a bit staged. Later in the show, Perot's 800 number flashed at the bottom of TV screens across the nation, and the switchboards began to light up. It wasn't long before hundreds of thousands of people called in, demanding a change in the way things were done in Washington.

Almost five million people responded; perhaps half a million became active volunteers. Perot simply didn't have the resources or the ability to organize them effectively. The campaign could not handle the extraordinary outpouring of support from the grass roots. This "instant" campaign was unprecedented in American history, and it was a harbinger of things to come.

Volunteers created their own organizations in fifty states, organizing themselves. As Tom Luce, Perot's campaign manager, recalled:

> There were only 50 people on the payroll of the campaign staff. Most of that number was totally absorbed in trying to deal with the byzantine FEC rules that required us to report everything. If a volunteer bought a billboard, we had to account for it. They were totally absorbed in explaining ballot-access rules in 50 states, how to comply with FEC rules, and refereeing intramural fights, but that's really all they did.

A large part of the problem was Perot himself. Perot, of course, had a lot of money and bragged initially that he'd spend a lot of it. But he parted with barely a fraction of it. Between March and July, he only spent $6 million, and he did not commit the resources necessary to building up an effective national organization. Still, he had enormous success in creating a presence on the national political stage.

As Luce explained after the election, "There was not a single signature paid for in that time period. As of July 16, when Perot withdrew, he had qualified on the ballot in 24 states. . . . There were enough signatures collected for him to qualify in another 16 at that point in time, so except in the state of New York, which was a problem later on, most of the ballot work had been done. It had been done by volunteers who organized their own effort."

Despite the lack of a national structure, a paucity of resources, and a candidate who acted inconsistently at best and erratically at worst, Perot's campaign had an unprecedented impact. The volunteers—hundreds, if not thousands, of them—conducted the ballot-access part of the effort efficiently. Perot's volunteers were typical of the people who got involved in independent politics at that time.

Bill Spiegel, 47, a Republican who had never been involved in a political campaign, signed on as a coordinator in Dade County, Florida. His wife, Betsy, and his brother, Bob, also volunteered. "Perot is giving me an opportunity to get involved the way I probably should have been all my life," Spiegel told *U.S. News & World Report*. "No matter what happens in this campaign, I will no longer be watching TV and wringing my hands."

"I don't give a damn what he thinks about abortion or gun control or fluoridation of water," added Mike Kelly, a volunteer in Colorado Springs, Colorado. "I know where he is on the deficit and I know he won't just talk a good game. He'll play it." In Wisconsin, Cindy Schultz organized coordinators in sixty-nine of the state's seventy-two counties, and ultimately mobilized 7,444 people to circulate petitions.

Huge numbers of volunteers joined, but the campaign did not have the tools to organize them. It installed a few computer systems, but it lacked sophisticated programs to manage all of its communications. The volunteers radiated enthusiasm and initiative, but did not jell into a smooth-functioning infrastructure. Perot simply did not have the resources, tools, or ability to use the hundreds of thousands of prospective volunteers who called his 800 number or his state campaign offices. There were too many logistical problems coordinating them and figuring out what they would do. A tool like the Internet would have helped immeasurably.

Despite these very considerable problems, Perot went from having virtually no support to garnering the leadership position in the polls in the four-month period between March and June 1992. His ascendance happened in large part because of the spontaneous outpouring of support he received. It was unprecedented in the annals of American history.

The world of politics has changed dramatically since then. Today, campaigns can use the Internet to organize and mobilize volunteers. They can also employ traditional mechanisms such as phone banks and door-to-door canvassers. They have integrated the older methods into a modern infrastructure built around computer networks that are supervised by technical wizards who can develop and tweak the software that ensures that the campaign is easily and instantly connected to the voters.

Volunteers still do the traditional tasks, but they can do far more on their own. Indeed, my experience has shown that the Internet can help people organize more effectively than ever before. They can participate in meet-ups, share files online, set up blogs, keep in touch by e-mail, and so on. They no longer need the campaign to catalyze mobilization or provide resources. There's a synergistic effect to all this that hasn't been fully realized or tested yet.

Perot's campaign was the beginning of something new at the grass roots, and the spontaneous volunteering and organizing in that 1992 effort led directly to Jesse Ventura's successful bid for the statehouse in Minnesota. Howard Dean also followed this model, using the Internet to organize his bid for the Oval Office.

Today, we have unprecedented anger and frustration. But we also have something else. We have the tools to build a national organization quickly and effectively and to raise the funds to run a campaign that could potentially dwarf the Perot effort in scope and impact. My analysis has shown that hundreds of thousands of people will readily respond to an independent candidate now. These individuals constitute a wellspring of potential energy waiting to be unleashed in the political arena. Perot helped change the way campaigns were run, as did Howard Dean. And if you thought Perot reached a critical mass of popularity quickly, that was just a preview. As you will see later in this chapter, the Barack Obama camp has enthusiastically embraced modern technology, enabling him to go from a first-term senator barely known outside of Illinois to a viable presidential candidate, initially leading in the Democrat fundraising race mostly because of the Internet. This took less than three months.

At this writing, we can't know how the 2008 campaign will play out. It's still far too early, and the field is crowded. But one thing is certain. It's not enough to base one's analysis on the predictable, the conventional wisdom. There is too much uncertainty. Technology is too powerful for us to underestimate what it can bring to a third-party or independent candidate.

My point is much broader, however. Certainly, it's about who will run and who will win. But it's also about *how* the candidates will run and talk to their supporters and voters. What issues will be on the nation's agenda? What does all this mean to you, the voter? How will you participate in today's new world of American democracy? Can you make a difference? It's my view that we will have the largest outpouring of political participation in a presidential election that we've ever seen. And by participation, I don't necessarily mean just turning out to vote. Rather, I mean volunteers participating in political campaigns in new and unexpected ways. For example, tens of thousands of people voted in the spring and summer of 2007 to help Hillary Clinton choose her campaign theme song. This is a far cry from what happened in 1996 when President Clinton asked me and a few other advisers what musical introduction he should have at the 1996 convention in Chicago. ("Don't Stop," by Fleetwood Mac, was ultimately chosen.)

The Romney campaign has actually posted video footage online and has called on Romney's supporters and potential supporters to work with that footage and footage that they gather themselves to help develop new ads for his campaign. This is a long way from what media consultants have traditionally done in expensive and secluded editing studios.

Volunteers can be mobilized faster than ever before. In 2005, Kevin Sheekey, one of the most creative campaign managers in America, mobilized almost sixty thousand volunteers in New York City for an election—Michael Bloomberg's run for his second term as mayor—that never appeared to be in serious doubt. Sheekey used the Internet, phone banks, and traditional advertising to mobilize more troops for Bloomberg than had volunteered for any other candidate for municipal office. He produced so many volunteer workers, in fact, that the city's media remained skeptical about the size, scope, and dimensions of Sheekey's army until they saw them out canvassing as election day approached.

Sheekey has speculated that, using the same techniques, he could mobilize between half a million and a million grassroots volunteers in key states should Mayor Bloomberg change his mind and decide to mount a campaign for the presidency.

Stephen Colbert's satirical candidacy for president may have fizzled out quickly when he was denied access to the South Carolina Democratic primary ballot, but it was not for lack of spontaneously generated support. Overall, 13 percent of American voters quickly said in a Rasmussen poll that they would support him in a three-way race with Hillary Clinton and Rudy Giuliani. A full 54 percent of Americans in a CNN poll said they believed he deserved a place on the South Carolina ballot. And on the Web, the outpouring of sympathy was even more dramatic. His Facebook political page attracted more than 1 million members in less than a week, making it more popular than any other candidate's group. The response was incredible, attracting an average of 83 new members a minute for eight days, forcing Facebook to take the page offline temporarily. The group's founder, Raj Vachhini, noted that it took Barack Obama more than a month to attract 380,000 members and Colbert recruited about twice as many in less than a week. Colbert's experience demonstrated that Sheekey is almost certainly on to something.

Ron Paul's insurgent campaign for the Republican nomination demonstrates how profoundly the Internet can affect the process. Once seen as a fringe candidate, Paul—a ten-term congressman who was also the Libertarian candidate for president in 1988—has won extraordinary amounts of support because of his online presence. His supporters raised, without his help or involvement, more than $4 million for his campaign in one day in early November, garnering, in Paul's words, $10 million in free publicity for his campaign. His online success led to a $1 million advertising campaign in Iowa and a dramatic improvement in his poll standing in New Hampshire. *The New York Times* concluded that, but for the Internet, there would not be a Paul candidacy:

> *If his campaign for President had taken place in the pre-Internet era, it might have gone the way of his 1988 Libertarian campaign for President, as a footnote to history. But because of the Internet's low-cost ability to connect grassroots supporters with one another—in this case, largely iconoclastic, white men—Mr. Paul's once-solo quest has taken on a life of its own. It is evolving from a figment of cyberspace into a traditional campaign.*

The new technology certainly has fundamentally altered the way our democracy works and the way people participate and obtain their information. In his memoir of the Howard Dean campaign, Joe Trippi wrote, "I believe that the Internet is the last hope for democracy." Trippi is almost certainly correct. The major issue now for candidates is marrying the technology to the campaign organization in a way that produces maximum benefit. Trippi added, "I believe the 2008 election will be the first national contest waged and won primarily over the Internet."

Because technology has empowered candidates and causes in ways that were impossible to predict just a few years ago, those candidates who take advantage of it will have a chance to make a greater impact in the future. Here's why.

First, the nature of political organizing has gone through a sea change in the past few years. Independents no longer think of themselves—and they refuse to be labeled—as "spoilers." This is a critical point in American politics today. The activists are independent; the people who worked for "Kinky" Friedman and Carole "Grandma" Strayhorn in the 2006 gubernatorial race proved it was possible to fundamentally alter a contest in a relatively conservative state, Texas. It's difficult to find reliable figures, but thousands of activist-organizers around the country are galvanizing a largely below-the-radar independent movement, separate and apart from individual campaigns.

As an analyst who has watched these changes over three decades, I think the promise and importance of this type of organizing is incalculable. There is now an independent infrastructure in place, providing a solid base for future candidates to build on. A candidate for national office can now quickly and easily draw on the resources of the state's network of activist-organizers and independents, who would most likely respond in large numbers to such an effort. You can mobilize volunteers and then they take on a life of their own. Organizing a political campaign can now be done from the bottom up, rather than the top down. Local groups can have their own meetings, their own fundraisers, and so on.

Second, the Internet is the most powerful tool ever conceived for organizing a campaign. It used to be that you had to go through what Perot went through in 1992; you wrote people's names on index cards, with their addresses and phone numbers, and so on. Then you hired a bunch of people with headsets and had them hit the phone banks. Now, with computers, blast e-mails, search engine optimizations, and interactive websites that serve specific demographics, you can build an organization from scratch. You can mobilize people to send e-mails to their friends; you can mobilize people to go to meet-ups. A campaign headquarters can be anywhere and everywhere. Supporters can track their candidate on a screen, any time of the day.

Third, a campaign organization's lifeblood is money. Without a steady flow of cash coming in, a candidate's chances can quickly fizzle. The Net has enabled organizers to reach supporters who can only afford to give small amounts. And the easiest way to do this is by clicking a button and using a credit card on the campaign website.

There is another source of volunteer activists that could also fundamentally alter the 2008 campaign, which is an organization called Unity08. Unity08 is a group of citizens recruited online, numbering now more than a hundred thousand people, who are deeply concerned that the two-party system has become unresponsive and who are committed to supporting a bipartisan third-party ticket in 2008. The organization was founded by Doug Bailey, Jerry Rafshoon, and Hamilton Jordan, Democrats and Republicans who have been involved at the highest levels of national and state government, as well as other activists, some of whom lack long experience in politics but share the organizers' belief that neither party reflects the will of the American people. The organization has mobilized these hundred thousand people and hopes to gather many more to hold an online primary as a means of choosing a bipartisan ticket to run for president. Unity08 is nonideological.

Unity08 wants the nominated candidate to focus on major issues like terrorism, debt, dependence on foreign oil, the emergence of India and China as strategic competitors, climate change, nuclear proliferation, and health care. Given the outpouring of support to the general idea of Unity08, the possibility of many more hundreds of thousands of people participating and potentially joining and ultimately supporting an independent candidate makes it a potentially potent force in the 2008 election.

When Ross Perot was running for president in 1992, few political experts could have predicted how the Internet would affect political campaigns, let alone a website like Independentvoting.org. In essence, the Perot campaign and movement was a protest against two-party politics. It was a protest against the blindness and the parochialism and the corruption that was ruling Washington. But the most important tool that the Perot campaign used to organize itself was an 800 number. Call me for free, Perot challenged, and the people responded. Today, the idea of asking voters to call in their support for free seems old-fashioned in comparison with the electronic power and resources we now have.

It no longer matters whether we're talking about Perot's Reform Party or an independent candidate. These tools are now cheaply available to all.

A number of websites seek to lure the independent voters who are looking for alternatives to the two-party system. These voters aren't "swing voters" who exist to be wooed and swayed by one or the other major party. These are people who have strongly held beliefs about how partisanship and ideological labeling are corrupting and constraining progress. They proudly defy traditional political labels; what they share is the genuine concern that we need major reforms of the electoral process.

Independents are building a constituency that demands to be heard; indeed, they have been steadily organizing among themselves. Listen to what one blogger, Sandylong5274, had to say: "Frankly, I have had it with both the sell-out Democratic and Republican Parties, and so I became an Independent after the GOP was crazy enough to nominate that pair of real losers George W. Bush and Draft Dodger Dickey Cheney! And as I look ahead towards Election Day 2008 I honestly do not see anyone from either party that I want to vote for. . . . It's high time we get a new third political party that serves the people . . ."

Another blogger, bobsnodgrass, wrote, "I have worked for Democratic candidates in the past but am increasingly angry and disillusioned with our political system. . . . I don't see any one of the current presidential candidates facing up to what I consider important issues, such as reducing military spending."

As this independent base grows, it will generate a more pressing call for political reform. Another blogger said, "The other problem with our system is the Electoral College. It is time to do away with it and elect our President by popular vote. That way a third-party candidate would have a fighting chance and more people would be able to vote for whom they believe in. I don't know about you, but I am getting damn sick and tired of voting for 'the lesser of two evils.' "

Candidates Ross Perot, Howard Dean, and Jesse Ventura were important because they raised public awareness about who could run—and potentially even win. But they left little in the way of an infrastructure for future campaigners who chose to eschew the Democratic and Republican parties. They ran, and they won or lost, and then their organizations disappeared from the public eye.

It's different today. "Independents don't want to join a third party," said Jackie Salit, a prominent national organizer of independent voters. "If you ask them, 'Will American democracy be strengthened by a third party?' fifty-seven percent will now tell you it will."

That's partly people expressing their dissatisfaction with the choices that are being presented by the two parties. "I see weaknesses in both parties, and even more so in the last fifteen years," said Donna Young of Sun City, Arizona, whose father was a Republican and whose mother was a Democrat. "I don't believe you can do justice to democracy if you only look at one particular party candidate."

The networks of independent organizers already in place would surprise most people, especially those who are confirmed Republicans or Democrats. There are people in organizations like Independent Texans, or IndependentVoice.org in California, or the Committee for an Independent Voice in New Hampshire, or the Independence Party in South Carolina (which is devoted to ballot access). You have the Sunshine Independents in Florida, the Independents in Oklahoma. The Minnesota Independence Party has been rebuilding itself since Jesse Ventura left office. During the last midterm election, such organizations helped statewide independent candidates do well in Massachusetts, Florida, and Illinois.

These organizations can be the seeds around the country that rapidly mobilize a presidential campaign. At this writing, some thirty-five state independent organizations participate in a regular conference call.

Betty Ward, a member of the New Hampshire Committee for an Independent Voice, articulates the perspective of many independents. She said, "I wish life was simple. I wish it was Republican, Democrat, black or white, yes or no. Life isn't that way. Situations in life need a broad base of thinking. You need to think out of the box, sometimes in the box, to the side of the box, on top of the box; you really have to have thinkers. You can't be narrow in solving problems and just having a narrow focus about philosophy. I just don't live my life that way. I never know what's out there or what's coming to my door, so I have to be open to any possibility. I feel that as an independent we need to look at problems more openly and be more receptive to what people have to bring to the table."

These sentiments of ordinary, intelligent voters are evident everywhere, and in the last midterm election such thinking had a profound effect in one of our largest states.

The Texas gubernatorial election in 2006 was important, not so much for the results (which were indeed surprising) but because two independents mounted bids in one of the states that make it most difficult to run as an independent candidate. Ballot access in Texas is made difficult because candidates cannot gather signatures from voters who have voted in a party primary that year. That cuts the available pool considerably.

Still, the two independent candidates, Carole Strayhorn and Kinky Friedman, managed to gather between 150,000 and 155,000 signatures each.

During the campaign, Strayhorn, who had been state comptroller, was polling at 20 to 25 percent, while Friedman got as high as the midteens. The Strayhorn campaign tried to convince Friedman to withdraw and throw his support to Strayhorn. Friedman's candidacy had started as something of a joke, but the popular country musician and novelist came to take the race more seriously than anyone would have thought. The offer was considered and ultimately declined.

Strayhorn and Friedman won a total of 1,344,446 votes, or 31 percent of the electorate. This was 34,691 votes more than the tally for the Democrat, Chris Bell, who came in second. The combined Strayhorn-Friedman vote was only 371,557 shy of the total of Republican governor Rick Perry, who won reelection with 1,716,803 votes, only 39 percent of the total turnout. This is a telling statistic. Most of the Texans who voted in the election voted for somebody other than the winner—and more voters chose the independents than the Democrat. This seismic shift in Texas politics has been underreported. The two-party system in the state suffered a severe jolt.

Carole Strayhorn carried 5 counties and came in second in 104 counties. The combined votes of Strayhorn and Friedman won 47 counties. What's more, the Southwest Voter Registration Education Project released some polling numbers (albeit perhaps methodologically flawed) indicating that Hispanic voters gave Chris Bell 39 percent of their votes, Strayhorn 29 percent, and Friedman 14 percent. Whatever the precise number, the fact that so many Hispanics "defected" from the major parties to independent candidates is a significant story in Texas.

Texas certainly put itself on the map with its refreshingly interesting campaign for governor, but it took a "flyover state" to truly define the modern era of campaign organizing.

The Internet will be remembered in politics first for the role it played in Jesse Ventura's successful run for the Minnesota governorship in 1998. Phil Noble was one of the seers who predicted that the Net would make a difference in a race that season. He famously (among political aides) made it known he'd bet a steak dinner that political organizing in cyberspace would win an election. "What's phenomenal is that we're sitting here debating whether a medium that did not exist four years ago won or lost a race," Noble told *The New York Times.*

During the campaign, Phil Madsen, the Web director for Ventura, used e-mail and Web instructions to show volunteers how to bring out the crowds in the towns where the candidate made campaign stops. Advancing made easy, you could say.

The campaign's final act was a seventy-two-hour drive through Minnesota that was organized and coordinated entirely by e-mail and through the campaign's website. You had to admire the moxie and the low-key, folksy touch of some of the communiqués. They are both typical of grassroots organizing on the Internet and emblematic of the kind of person who wanted to see an insurgent candidate pull off an upset victory.

One example was published in *The New York Times:* "Friday night we will be going from bar to bar in the Northern Metro area: Champs on I-35E and Larpentuer, the Eagles Club in New Brighton, the Mermaid in Moundsview, and the Be-Bop in Blaine. Jesse will spend 20 to 30 minutes at each stop. No drinking and driving if you are with us on the caravan. We mean it. . . . If you do, you will likely find yourself spending the night in jail. If that happens, and since you won't have much else to do anyway, see what you can do to get your arresting officer and detox cell mates to vote for Jesse on Tuesday!"

E-mails like that proved decisive for Ventura, according to Phil Madsen. "How else are you going to pull together 250 people in 36 hours?" Soon after the rallies ended, the campaign's "geek squad" posted digital photos on the Ventura website. "By the time you got home from the rally," Madsen said, "you could see a picture of yourself in the crowd." It seems like a minor conceit, but it points to the immediacy of participatory democracy in today's fast-paced world. In future campaigns, this type of communication and interaction will become de rigueur. Perhaps every voter will get his or her fifteen minutes of (modest) fame, after all.

It's no secret among political pundits that Ventura's stunning success was an inspiration for the same type of organizing on the national level. In that spirit, the Howard Dean campaign was unique in 2004. Dean was virtually unknown beyond his home state of Vermont, where he was governor. And because of savvy organizers who saw the power of the Internet, the campaign raised Dean's media profile and name recognition perhaps faster than any other such effort in American history. If it hadn't been for the World Wide Web, Dean's name would be buried in political obscurity. His campaign eventually imploded on the sour note of a media slip, but at least he will be more than a mere footnote.

Early on, the Dean for America site linked to Meetup.com.

The Dean supporters quickly grew to 2,700 members. This permanent link cost the campaign only a one-time $2,500 fee. (This might turn out to be the all-time bargain Internet buy in modern politics.) "We fell into this by accident," Dean told *Wired* magazine. "I wish I could tell you we were smart enough to figure this out. But the community taught us. They seized the initiative through Meetup. They built our organization for us before we had an organization."

The Bush campaign in 2004 also used the Internet skillfully to augment its formidable organizing effort. By organizing neighborhoods and precincts based on existing information and data, the incumbent was able to outorganize John Kerry and get a disproportionately large number of his own supporters to the polls on election day, confounding the experts who thought that the bulk of the energy and enthusiasm in the 2004 election lay with the Democrats.

In 2004, the Bush campaign was perceived after the fact as the state of the art. But individual, local efforts have actually gone beyond what the Bush campaign was able to do that year. To date, probably the most successful use of the Internet for a targeted voter outreach initiative was the one we organized in the 2001 and 2005 mayoral campaigns of New York City's Mike Bloomberg. In those efforts, we were able to segment the electorate down to the individual level and determine how voters were likely to think about politics based on information gathered from interviewing them in detail over the phone. We were also able to use this information to categorize voters into clusters and communicate targeted messages based on their shared interests and attributes. The result was a campaign that operated largely below the radar and won an upset victory in 2001 and a landslide of nearly 60 percent in 2005.

As discussed, there would have been no Ned Lamont without the Internet. Lamont was an unknown wealthy businessman who was unhappy with the way Joe Lieberman represented Connecticut in the Senate, and particularly with his support for the war in Iraq. Far more significant than Lamont's primary victory, however, was his campaign's power to organize and mobilize a constituency against a powerful incumbent, making critical use of a constituency group that until Howard Dean's campaign in 2004 had simply not been recognized by bloggers and online activity.

In the aftermath of Lamont's successful campaign to win the Democratic nomination, *Time* magazine concluded correctly that "the gang of liberal bloggers and online activists who helped raise millions of dollars for Howard Dean's presidential campaign two years ago are now said to be Democratic kingmakers."

Lamont's aides set up a rudimentary webpage with the goal of amassing 1,000 volunteers in all 169 of the state's municipalities, building on the strength of local Democratic organizations. The campaign used a voter-history project to recruit those who had voted in every local primary and referendum, no matter how small or insignificant. This was extremely valuable because that information was not readily available in statewide voter rolls. This initiative probably would have been impossible—or at least it would have taken far longer—had it not been for the Internet.

One crucial part of campaign organizing is fundraising, and in this the Internet has showed astonishing mettle not only for campaigns but also for more focused political efforts:

• Both Barack Obama and Ron Paul have raised a large percentage of their campaign funds online—probably well in excess of a majority for Paul, who raised a record $4 million online in a single day, November 5. Obama, who has raised at least seven or eight times what Paul has garnered overall, has managed to collect at least a quarter of his financial support over the Web.

- "Netroots" activists helped build support for Virginia's new Democratic senator, Jim Webb (a former Republican), in the early days of his 2006 race. In one eighteen-hour period, Webb's Internet-based political action committee raised $500,000 online to buy airtime for advertising that targeted Republicans in four congressional races as well as supporting his own candidacy.

- ActBlue, an online clearinghouse that has raised more than 30 million since 2004, allows voters to contribute to any Democratic candidate for federal office and for many state offices.

- ABCPac's Rightroots, a Republican website started in September 2006, raised $300,000 for House and Senate candidates in the 2006 election. This political action committee simply followed ActBlue's lead, declaring that it will raise money to draft future presidential contenders.

- MoveOn.org Political Action raised $500,000 online to buy airtime for advertising for Democrats in four 2006 congressional races. "The presidential race that's coming up is one where online fundraising has the power to completely level the playing field," said Eli Pariser, executive director of MoveOn.

- Retired navy vice admiral Joe Sestak played the Internet money card to defeat incumbent Republican representative Curt Weldon and gain a House seat from the Philadelphia suburbs. He raised more money than his opponent largely because of nearly $900,000 in online contributions. Sestak confessed that he had no clue about the role the Web would play in the race when he announced his candidacy. He learned quickly, however. After he called for troop withdrawals in Iraq, his position resonated with netroots activists opposed to the war. He sent this message to liberal bloggers at the first YearlyKos, the convention hosted by the liberal political weblog Daily Kos. The Web became "an absolutely critical source" of money, Sestak said. In one four-day period, a single e-mail solicitation raised $88,000.

When Vermont independent Bernie Sanders ran for Congress in 1988, he cited the small contributors as making a difference. He said that he received tens of thousands of individual contributions. Some were as little as $5; some were $20. These small contributions—eight thousand in all—enabled Sanders to raise enough money to withstand what was one of the most vigorous negative campaigns ever run in Vermont.

Candidates of every political stripe are altering their strategies to collect the $20, $30, and $50 donations needed in the aftermath of the changes to campaign-finance laws in 2002 that banned large donations. Online fundraising has proved a cost-effective, efficient, and fast way to raise cash and organize the troops. It has already had an impact in transforming fundraising in presidential races. (It's difficult to quantify Internet contributions in campaigns because candidates and political parties are not required to disclose which donations came via the Web, but estimates show that the amount is fairly significant.)

Democrats Barack Obama and John Edwards have garnered roughly a third of their donations on the Net, mostly in small amounts. And many donors are repeat givers. Obama's campaign organization appears to have adopted the social-networking sites as primary organizing tools, which begets supporters who open their wallets to the cause. His website has generated more than 10,000 "events," where people come together virtually or in person, as early as eight months before the first 2008 primary. Obama has 136,000 "friends" on MySpace and 102,000 on Facebook. Count on these numbers to be growing steadily even as I write this.

Obama's own website helped to gather more than 350,000 donors and more than half a million donations as of October 2007. He brought in $32.5 million in donations in the second quarter of 2007; a large amount of this money came in contributions of $100 or less. This is what can be done, and it's just the tip of the iceberg.

The presidential campaign of 2008 is ushering in the phenomenon of the "microbundler." This is a direct descendant of the "bundling" that George Bush used so successfully in his last two campaigns: fat cats who were significant Bush campaign donors would call up ten or twenty of their friends and associates and ask for contributions. Now that dynamic has given way to a completely different paradigm. Camille Rey, a thirty-eight-year-old professional from San Jose, California, told *The New York Times* that she had become enamored of Barack Obama. She first contributed $50 online, and made some subsequent smaller donations. But then she constructed a fundraising page on the campaign's website. She e-mailed forty of her friends and relatives, asking them to contribute and to replicate the process that she went through by setting up additional fundraising pages for their own friends and relatives. The result has been an almost unprecedented number of donors and supporters for the Illinois senator's campaign.

"It's inevitable that the Internet will become the principal means of fundraising from now on," Anthony Corrado, a campaign finance expert at Colby College in Waterville, Maine, said in *USA Today.* "It's the only way you get a million people to each give you $10 on the same day."

The future of political organizing includes the previously mentioned bold new experiment Unity08, which will hold the first-ever presidential nominating convention *online*. Each delegate, or any registered voter who joins Unity08 online, will vote for the candidate he or she wants to run as an independent in the 2008 election.

The Unity08 website has been masterfully designed to be fantastically interactive. Its primary mission is to encourage site visitors to become involved with the presidential campaign in a unique way. The "Take Action" menu on the Unity08 website invites viewers to "Become a Member," "Volunteer," "Tell Your Friends," download "Unity08 Banners for Your Website," or create your own "Dream Ticket." It also asks viewers to help with ballot access across the country and to become involved on college campuses (if they are students). Many possible candidates exist. Among those mentioned by Doug Bailey, a Unity08 founder: Al Gore, Colin Powell, Bill Gates, and Tom Brokaw.

But candidates won't simply be drafted without their consent. Unity08 promises not to conscript anyone who won't consider running under its banner.

What's also unique about the organization is that it's welcoming candidates from either party (or independents) to seek the convention nomination. Unity08 will allow them to campaign right on the website. The candidates can use the available technology and bring in their own gadgets as well—streaming video of their positions on the crucial issues, daily blogs, online debates among the candidates, and any other method they can come up with to creatively express their views and platforms. On the convention ballot each delegate will vote for one "Unity Ticket" (just as presidents and vice presidents are elected as a team in November). There will be as many convention ballots as are needed until one Unity Ticket wins at least 51 percent of all delegates voting.

This is an ambitious test for representative democracy, and if it is even modestly successful, it will make a fundamental difference in upcoming presidential elections. Unity08's delegates have initiated the first-ever "national presidential caucus," in which thousands of local, *self-organized,* Web-enabled, and face-to-face gatherings will convene in thousands of cities and small towns across America on December 7, 2007. Then there will be a "national primary," scheduled for February 5, 2008, when two presidential candidates emerge, based on input from the site's delegates.

Doug Bailey puts it this way: "The National Presidential Caucus is a fabulous way to let the people back into the process. It's a straw vote when you don't even have to be bused across the country to Ames, Iowa, to take part. Imagine that—the voice of the real people might actually be heard."

It started in the early 1990s with an 800 number. Now we have low-cost communications that allow anyone with a head for organizing to practically invent a candidate overnight.

We now have the tools to organize a campaign that can succeed on a far greater scale than even Joe Trippi envisioned. People are looking for a candidate; they're hungering for someone who shares their ideals. This is why there's been such an outpouring of support for an idea like Unity08, which is mobilizing that sentiment at a frenetic pace. Almost spontaneously, a massive force could emerge that will make the Perot campaign look like the twentieth-century version of the Boston Tea Party.

7

Ballot Access Has Been Democratized

*There are two ways to defeat democracy, one way is by preventing
citizens from voting, and the other is by preventing worthy
candidates from appearing on the ballot.*

—*American Chronicle,* June 28, 2005

IN THE HEAT OF THE 2004 CAMPAIGN, RALPH NADER CALLED DEMO-
cratic National Committee chairman Terry McAuliffe. He was
angry, to say the least, and it was a terribly awkward phone conversation. As Nader crisscrossed the country, drumming up support for his candidacy, he encountered numerous instances when
his volunteers claimed that Democratic operatives were systematically harassing those who were collecting signatures to get
Nader on the ballot.

Nader told McAuliffe he'd heard of an organized campaign to
keep him from running in several key states. It even had a name:
the Ballot Project. He wanted to know if there was any truth to it.

McAuliffe admitted that he knew about it, and in fact endorsed it.

Nader was incredulous. He'd already complained to Senator

John Kerry about this underground initiative. The Democratic candidate promised to look into it. Nader was waiting to hear back.

McAuliffe said he was serious. There were thirty-one states that the Democrats had already deemed either "red" or "blue." You can campaign there, McAuliffe told Nader, and we won't bother you. In fact, we'll even withdraw our petition challenges. But in the other nineteen states, those up for grabs, we're going to come after you, he intimated.

McAuliffe made good on his pledge.

Kerry never called Nader back.

Almost everything that's wrong with the ballot-access process can be gleaned from Ralph Nader's struggle to reach the voters of Pennsylvania, a key 2004 battleground state. It was emblematic of the problems that fringe candidates face in presidential elections. After the 2000 election, when every Democratic operative publicly blamed Nader for bleeding votes from Gore and throwing the contest to Bush, the party leadership did not want to see a repeat performance in the Kerry-Bush contest. Terry McAuliffe became the bane of the Nader campaign.

Here's how Project Ballot worked: Democrats sued the Nader campaign in twelve Pennsylvania courts to restrict its ballot access. The law firm of Reed Smith has disclosed that it did this work for the Democratic Party pro bono. Reed Smith estimated that it spent more than $4 million to prevent Pennsylvania citizens from voting for a third-party candidate. I'm sure you'll agree that this isn't the kind of democracy the Founding Fathers had in mind. Nader had to gather nearly 27,000 signatures to qualify for the ballot, so staffers placed ads in Philadelphia newspapers seeking people to circulate petitions.

What happened next resembled the dirty tricks and hysteria of the Watergate era. According to a 2005 article in *American Chronicle:*

*As the law suits were unfolding one of the Nader campaign work-
ers parked his car . . . outside of Nader headquarters. . . . A person who is now unidentified pulled up . . . and asked if indeed he
was with the Nader campaign. When he responded in the affir-
mative this unidentified driver then said to him, "You know what
happened to you here in Philadelphia don't you." The Nader
worker said "No, what?" He was then told that "you people were
paying a dollar per valid signature but the mayor's office is paying
two dollars to forge each name. Now we got you," he continued,
"now you're going to have to go into court, present these signatures
and you'll have to claim that they are valid and since you didn't
pay us for them, now we're going to sue you because they're invalid."*

In the end, Pennsylvania authorities reviewed 51,273 petition
signatures and disqualified nearly two-thirds (32,455) of them
(although only 1.3 to 1.4 percent were deemed flat-out fraudulent). Nader was disqualified from the Pennsylvania ballot because he didn't obtain the minimum number of valid signatures,
although he submitted nearly twice as many as were needed.
Adding insult to injury, one court ruled that he couldn't qualify as
an independent candidate because he was already on the Florida
ballot as the Reform Party candidate.

An angry Nader charged that the Pennsylvania shenanigans
represented just the tip of the iceberg of Democratic dirty tricks.
Democrats were quite organized and willing to disrupt his campaign, he said. At a press conference at the National Press Club in
Washington in September 2004, he complained bitterly that the
party was subverting the democratic process. "In state after state,
they're promoting an unprecedented dirty tricks campaign
against us," he said. "That's to put it mildly. Dozens of phony lawsuits requiring our signature guys to appear in court on short notice with all kinds of records going back to 2000. We are moving

to quash the subpoenas, and we have won about nine out of 11 state Supreme Court decisions that put us back on the ballot. There's intimidation and harassment."

Among the examples of harassment that Nader cited was that of a fifty-eight-year-old woman in Portland, Oregon, who spent her days collecting signatures. One day, she went back home and cooked dinner for her grandchildren and there was a knock on the door. A well-dressed man and woman appeared and told her that if her petitions contained fraudulent signatures, she could be prosecuted and sent to jail for three years. Needless to say, she became terrified about doing anything more on the campaign. Such intimidation discouraged an additional thirty signature gatherers just in the Portland area.

Nader also accused the Democrats of employing three corporate law firms to hassle his campaign in Arizona. In one instance, the firms claimed that an ex-felon had collected 550 of Nader's petition signatures, rendering the signatures invalid because the ex-felon (who had been rehabilitated and was on jury duty) owed the state of Arizona $400.

The Democrats hired Kirkland, Ellis, a large, well-known corporate law firm, to go after Nader's campaign in Ohio. Nader claimed the firm had fifty lawyers in Ohio seeking to invalidate his petitions. The chairwoman of the Maine Democratic Party acknowledged that the Democratic National Committee footed the bill for her time and lawyers to keep Nader off the ballot in her state.

Nader emphasized that he wasn't welcomed in the presidential race by either party. With Bush up for reelection, the Republicans weren't taking any chances, either. While Democratic Party operatives spearheaded the challenge against Nader, corporate operatives with links to the Republicans also worked to stymie him. As Nader summarized the issue at the National Press Club:

What I'm saying to both parties: get off our backs, stop entangling us in your insidious schemes, let us compete for the voters. All of this is designed not just to get us off the ballot in numerous states that are considered close by the Democratic Party, but to deny millions of voters the opportunity to vote for the Nader-Camejo ticket, a rather serious civil liberties issue because the essence of running for office is freedom of speech, petition and assembly. It's remarkable how the civil liberties establishment could care less. They could care less about ballot access, period, with very few exceptions.

McAuliffe and Nader locked horns in a total of sixteen states, paralyzing the campaign of the famous consumer advocate. In the end, he couldn't fight the party machines.

It was reminiscent of what happened in 1980 to John Anderson, whose campaign withered when he was shut out of the final debate. Anderson, however, did not face the same ballot-access issues as other third-party candidates. His problems had different causes, such as fundraising shortfalls. Anderson eventually ended up on the ballot in all fifty states and the District of Columbia, but his campaign ultimately proved underpowered, undermanned, and underfinanced.

Ralph Nader's 2004 Pennsylvania experience underscores the challenge of ballot access. Ballot-access issues like those faced by Nader in 2004 and (to a lesser extent) in 2000 and by John Anderson in 1980 can block the successful launching and execution of an independent campaign. But if a ballot-access effort mobilizes tens or hundreds of thousands of volunteers, it can empower, embolden, and strengthen a campaign, as it did in the case of Ross Perot. Perot's campaign failed organizationally because it lacked tools to marshal the support it had. But his ballot-access effort, which was mounted with relatively limited resources and very limited coordination with the national headquarters, demonstrated the power and potency of Perot's appeal.

In 2008, the power of the Internet and the strength of the Unity08 organization could mobilize hundreds of thousands of volunteers on behalf of a compelling, centrist, nonpartisan alternative candidacy. Even so, the two major parties undoubtedly will conspire to keep any independent candidate off the ballots in the battleground states.

Historically, our two major political parties have made it notoriously difficult for maverick candidates to gain ballot access for a presidential run. Each state presents a gauntlet of different requirements, application forms, and filing dates—both collection windows and deadlines—for races, even national ones.

A serious independent presidential candidate would have to retain a staff of lawyers just to handle the ballot-access challenges and lawsuits he or she could expect from the major parties. Unless an independent garnered an overwhelming number of signatures, far above the required minimums, he or she could expect court challenges by either the Democratic or the Republican candidate (or both), on the theory that an independent can siphon votes and become a spoiler. It's to the two parties' advantage to team up and stifle any upstart challengers, whether from the Green Party, the Reform Party, or an independent. The greater the number of electoral votes a state has, the more important that state is.

"The United States is the only Western democracy in which the political process is controlled by two major parties," Chi Chi Sileo and Lisa Leiter of *Insight* magazine wrote a little more than a decade ago. "In other countries, including even some of the newly emerging democracies, election rules make it easy for alternative parties to get on the ballots and provide more choices."

In Britain, our mother country, every candidate for Parliament faces the same ballot-access hurdle: a simple filing fee. Candidates, regardless of their party affiliation, are granted one free mailing to all the voters, and every party gets a certain amount of free TV and radio time. There is thus legal parity among all the parties. And, no surprise, Britain has developed a healthy three-party system.

Ballot access is improving, however, as smaller parties and independents become savvier and learn to work the system. Today, only a handful of states make it extremely tough on third-party and independent candidates. Modern mobilization techniques and professional signature-gathering organizations make it easier. If you need 50,000 petition bearers in Harris County, Texas, you can get them. If you're having a problem in Wichita, you can solve it.

Technology has made it simpler for candidates to canvass neighborhoods and gather signatures. Using the Internet to rally supporters, campaign organizers can quickly identify and mobilize canvassers and cover the neighborhoods that will yield the best results.

In particular, technology can help in a state like Texas. In Texas, a presidential candidate must collect 75,000 signatures between March 12 and May 12 of a presidential election year. Any signature obtained before or after those cutoff dates is summarily disqualified. State law also mandates that petition signers cannot have voted in any primary. Jackie Salit, an independent organizing expert, put it this way: "I've run statewide campaigns in Texas, ballot access campaigns, and they're awful, truly one of the worst experiences in electoral politics." Numerous court challenges have sought to expand the petitioning period and gain other concessions, but so far the legislature has resisted reform.

Forty years ago, it took an all-out effort to mobilize a campaign to get a third-party candidate into contention for a presidential election. The most spectacular popular participation in presidential politics outside the two-party framework got George Wallace on the ballots of all fifty states in 1968, when impediments to ballot access were much more onerous than they are today. In California, Wallace had to obtain 66,000 signatures—not a daunting number, but in 1967 every person signing had to fill out a two-page legal-size form. In Ohio, he had to get the absurd total of 433,000—in just ten weeks. In November, he won only 13.5 percent of the vote, but carried five southern states with 45 electoral votes. With today's technology helping campaign organizers, getting a Wallace on the ballot would be much easier. That campaign would be free to worry about the more important issues.

You probably recall the famous free-for-all that followed California's recall of Governor Gray Davis in the fall of 2003. To launch a candidacy, one needed only to collect 65 signatures and to pay a filing fee of $3,500. As a result, 247 hopefuls attempted to get on the ballot, and 135 actually ran. The proliferation of candidacies confused the electorate; even the most civic-minded citizens couldn't keep track of the qualifications and views of that many candidates. But the special election was probably the modern high-water mark for open democracy in any state. (Former bodybuilder and action-film star Arnold Schwarzenegger prevailed, and he's generally received positive reviews, exceeding the expectations of most doubters.)

For greater ballot-access reform we'd have to go back a hundred years. In the nineteenth century, ballot-access laws did not impede third-party candidates. Ballot-access laws, where they existed at all, encouraged both independent candidates and third-party candidates. We had a healthy, flourishing two-party system in which several major parties came into and went out of existence. In 1854, the newly founded Republican Party won more governor's seats and sent more representatives to the House than did any other party. (There were no ballot-access laws until 1888. During the nineteenth century voter turnout ran about 80 percent.)

In the nineteenth century, the concept of public financing of the two major parties didn't exist. It began only in 1974, with an amendment to the Federal Election Campaign Act. Since then, the Democrats and the Republicans have in part financed presidential campaigns with taxpayer money. Under the 1974 law, no third-party candidate in a general election has ever received public funding, although a handful of third-party presidential candidates have been granted some primary funds.

Some ballot-access requirements are, of course, necessary; otherwise, we'd have a California recall situation almost everywhere there's a ballot box. From the advent of preprinted ballots in 1890 through 2005, there have only been two cases in which a ballot for federal or state office has had more than ten candidates, provided that at least 2,500 signatures were required to get on the ballot (and even in those cases, there were twelve or fewer candidates).

Still, it's notoriously difficult for candidates to get on the ballot in New York, Alabama, Maryland, and Florida. By contrast, in Louisiana and Arkansas, only a few hundred signatures and a nominal filing fee are required. If you want to be considered in all fifty states and the District of Columbia, you'll need a cadre of lawyers, not to mention a substantial amount of money to stave off the inevitable lawsuits and court challenges.

If you believe in open forums, fair elections, and true democracy, you have to feel some sympathy for Nader's plight four years ago, when he was kicked off the ballot in Virginia, Illinois, Maryland, Pennsylvania, and Missouri. In each case, officials said that Nader campaign workers either did not submit enough valid signatures on their petitions or failed to follow proper procedures. Virginia invalidated Nader's petitions on the grounds that the signatures weren't grouped according to district. (In 2000, when Nader had a far greater impact on the election results, he was denied ballot access in five *different* states: North Carolina, Georgia, Indiana, Oklahoma, and Idaho.)

Many states mandate that the number of signatures required on both presidential-primary and independents' petitions must correspond to a certain percentage of the votes cast in the previous election. In those states, the number of required signers varies from year to year. In Arizona and Michigan, for example, the required number of signatures went up sharply because voter turnout increased in 2006 over 2002. West Virginia will have a higher signature threshold in 2008 because turnout in 2004 was much higher than in 2000.

Thus, the greater the participation in our electoral system, the harder it frequently is for an independent candidate to get on the ballot. This anomaly must be addressed in any political reform package.

If you are an independent presidential candidate considering a run in 2008, your staff must long have focused on the minutiae of each state's ballot requirements. The staff will have to aggressively attack the ballot-access issue in all swing states. For the 2008 contest, nine states—which represent a total of 49 electoral votes—require that an independent presidential candidate not be registered as a member of a political party in order to run as an independent.

TABLE 2. **Dates a Candidate Must Disaffiliate to Appear on the 2008 Ballot as an Independent Candidate (Chronological)**

COLORADO	Must be registered by June 17, 2007 (one year before filing deadline).
MASSACHUSETTS	Must be registered by October 5, 2007 (one year before primary eligibility for major-party candidates).
OREGON	Must be registered by February 27, 2008.
MAINE	Must be registered by March 1, 2008.
PENNSYLVANIA	Must be registered by March 2, 2008 (one month before primary).
DELAWARE	Must be registered by June 1, 2008 (three months before required declaration of candidacy).
KANSAS	Must be registered by August 4, 2008.
ALASKA	Must be registered by August 6, 2008.
IDAHO	Must be registered by August 25, 2008.

According to the most current research, the most challenging ten states for ballot access—representing 192 electoral votes, or more than two-thirds of the total required to win the presidency—for independent candidates considering a 2008 run are the following:

TABLE 3. **Most Challenging States for Ballot Access,
in Chronological Order**

TEXAS	75,000 signatures between March 12 and May 12, 2008; petition signers cannot have voted in a primary.
CALIFORNIA	158,000 signatures from registered voters between April 25 and August 8, 2008.
PENNSYLVANIA	49,000 signatures between March 6 and August 1, 2008; will have to disaffiliate from a major party by January.
MICHIGAN	30,000 signatures but cannot submit more than 60,000 signatures (meaning there is very little margin for error for a campaign if some invalid signatures are submitted).
NORTH CAROLINA	70,000 signatures by June 27, 2008; start date unclear.
GEORGIA	49,000 signatures between February 6 and August 4, 2008; must declare candidacy by August 1, 2008.
OKLAHOMA	44,000 signatures by July 15, 2008; petitions must be circulated by Oklahoma residents.
OREGON	19,000 signatures required by June 17, 2008; may have to disaffiliate from a major party by January 2008.
COLORADO	5,000 signatures required by June 17, 2007; may have to disaffiliate by June 2007.
MASSACHUSETTS	10,000 signatures required by August 25, 2008; may have to disaffiliate by October 2007.

Four states—Colorado, Oregon, Massachusetts, and Pennsylvania—make both lists. In all, fifteen states can be called potential "trouble" states (in addition to the four mentioned earlier—New York, Alabama, Maryland, and Florida) for any candidate willing to challenge the two-party juggernaut in 2008. In my view, nineteen states pose significant challenges for any independent candidate who wants to get on the ballot (although not all of them will be that difficult for the campaign with a well-prepared staff).

In all, any candidate wishing to get on the ballot in all fifty states and the District of Columbia will need a minimum of 792,763 valid signatures—which means collecting a lot more in order to be safe.

The good news is that there are a substantial number of court cases and bills pending in several states in dire need of ballot-access reform, and bills have recently passed in other states. Alabama is perhaps the most noteworthy. The Alabama House Constitution and Elections Committee passed a bill in April 2007 that moved the state a step closer to real political reform. It mandates that the state's presidential electors be elected proportionately to the state's popular vote. Only two other states, Maine and Nebraska, have adopted this far more equitable format for choosing a president. Had it been in effect in Alabama in 2004, President Bush would have received 6 electoral votes and Senator Kerry would have been awarded 3, instead of Bush receiving all 9. Not enough to change the outcome of the election—but imagine what would have happened if all the other states had used this method. I'll speak more to the issue of political reform in the last chapter.

In at least ten other states various legislative initiatives and court tests should result in a far less hostile environment for third-party candidates.

Note Michigan's minimum and maximum requirements for signatures (see Table 3), which make qualifying for the ballot much more difficult, because a candidate can fail to qualify if a relatively small number of signatures are disallowed for technical reasons. One of the most common weapons a party uses to disqualify a candidate from a state ballot is to challenge the petitions and signatures through the secretary of state's office in the state, and ultimately, in court—the approach McAuliffe used against Nader in Pennsylvania. Examining and verifying the signatures can take weeks and exhaust a candidate's financial and human resources. (There are court cases pending to decide who pays for this—the candidate's campaign, as is now the case, or the taxpayers. Nader's campaign has received hefty bills for some of these costs, and the courts have upheld them. The appeals process can go on for years.) Anticipating this problem, independent candidates usually submit far more than the required number, expecting a certain percentage of disqualifications and in hopes of discouraging lawsuits challenging the petitions submitted.

The validity of a signature can be questioned in numerous ways, ranging from "illegibility" to the fact that the petitioner did not display the proper credentials. The challenges can be based on ludicrous criteria: printed instead of signed signatures, address information written in the hand of someone who did not sign the petition, registration at an address other than the one on the petition, use of nicknames or initials, various affidavit problems, almost any clerical error, and so on.

If the previous presidential election is any gauge, expect the lawyers to be busy from summer to fall if an independent is a serious factor in the race. In October 2004, Ballot Access News, a website devoted to covering such issues, reported that there were sixteen losses, nine wins, and six cases still pending in courts around the nation in cases involving expanding ballot access. It's not encouraging to know that some cases can drag on after election day, rendering them moot. So even if you eventually "win," you still "lose." Republicans and Democrats customarily file suits even when they know there's no chance of winning them.

The major parties, of course, have mechanisms all over the nation to try to limit insurgent campaigns. But more and more we're seeing countervailing energy and resources that make it easier to strike back and challenge the status quo.

You have to admire the voters of New Hampshire, who take seriously the state's motto, "Live Free or Die." New Hampshire may be the nation's most fiercely independent state. There, the Committee for an Independent Voice twice defeated, in 2005 and again in 2007, an effort by the legislature to constrain the right of independents to vote in open primaries.

In New Hampshire, 44 percent of the electorate is registered as independent. The independent bloc there is serious and well organized.

The two-party regime in New Hampshire tried to fight this trend. The legislature introduced a bill requiring independents who want to vote in party primaries to register as party members at least ninety days before the primary. They'd then have to go to their local board of registrars in order to reregister as an independent. Happily, the bill failed. The Committee for an Independent Voice, comprising maybe fifteen or twenty activists all over the state, called hundreds of independents and persuaded them to send letters and e-mails and make phone calls to their local elected officials. The measure was killed in committee. New Hampshire's citizenry is determined to have the people decide the outcome of their elections. The 44 percent of the electorate who are committed independents are now able to have their say.

Right now, if you're an independent, you can go to the polls in New Hampshire, and you can vote in whichever primary you want. You can exit the polling booth and sign a paper that says "I'm still an independent." And it's been that way since 1910. The Democrats and Republicans in New Hampshire were so worried about the growth of the independent sector that they tried to change the law, basically to use it as a party-building tool. The independents successfully resisted it.

As soon as the entrenched political powers in New Hampshire realized that independents were asserting their political interests, they understood that they didn't want to end up on the wrong side of those voters.

I believe that in upcoming ballot-access fights in many more states, many politicians will come to the same realization. The momentum appears to be shifting away from the stifling requirements that frustrate both candidates and voters, who are demanding more choices on the first Tuesday in November. My prediction is that as the independent movement grows, as more disaffected Republicans and Democrats abandon their parties, pressure will mount on state legislatures to further ease ballot-access impediments. When the number of unaffiliated voters exceeds 40 percent—how far away can that be?—then maybe we'll see real change in the process we create to allow candidates to contend for the nation's highest office.

8

A Different Kind of Presidential Debate

*The debate commission should be broadened to include third-party
members and independents and others, or it should be replaced. The
two major parties are becoming so much alike, and the American people know it. They want more choices. Maybe if we let other people participate in the debates, people will start believing that politics matters.*

—Congressman John Lewis, former member of the
Commission on Presidential Debates

*The purpose of the Commission, it seems to me, is to try to preserve
the two-party system that works very well, and if you like the multiparty system, then go to Sri Lanka and India and Indonesia.
I think it's obvious that independent candidates mess things up.*

—Alan Simpson, director of the Commission
on Presidential Debates in 2002

It was prime time, and it was perhaps the reality show of the
season. On the evening of Monday, July 23, 2007, the people of
this country seized the podium, shoved aside the professional
journalist moderators, and asked the Democratic presidential
candidates their own questions. Individual Americans submitted
some three thousand "video questions" for consideration at the
debate co-sponsored by CNN and YouTube; of those, thirty-nine
were eventually broadcast and responded to by the candidates
who assembled in Charleston, South Carolina.

It was a novel idea, and one that was long overdue. If the YouTube debate is any indication, and I believe it is, presidential debates are moving toward an interactive model—one in which the voters will influence who participates and what the questions are. This format contrasts with the elite-driven, top-down model the Commission on Presidential Debates has imposed in past elections.

This change has enormous implications for an independent candidate for president because the whole process of organizing and planning debates has to be fundamentally changed if the voices of independent candidates are to be fully reflected in the national dialogue. Indeed, unless an independent can participate in the 2008 presidential debates, not only can he not win, but he probably cannot even be a factor in the election. A look back at prior elections demonstrates conclusively why this is the case.

The Commission on Presidential Debates (CPD) was formed in 1988 by the Democratic and Republican parties, and its heads (both former chairmen of the Democratic National Committee and the Republican National Committee) have systematically tried to limit participation to the candidates of the two major parties. It is no surprise that when Ross Perot was finally allowed to participate in 1992 after much wrangling, viewership went up and Perot's poll standings nearly doubled overnight to close to the 20 percent he ultimately received, based in large part on his strong performance in those debates. By contrast, in 1996, when he was excluded, viewership and interest plummeted and Perot's vote share remained in single digits through election day. Similarly, Ralph Nader was excluded from both the 2000 and 2004 presidential debates, despite popular support for his inclusion. As a result, he was never able to realize the potential support polls suggested he could achieve if voters thought he had a realistic chance of winning—especially in the 2000 election, when some estimates suggested that he could under some circumstances get as much as 10 percent of the vote.

Perot's 1992 experience was mirrored by Jesse Ventura in his 1994 campaign for governor of Minnesota. He was polling about 10 percent before his debates with former Minnesota attorney general Hubert H. Humphrey III, and former St. Paul mayor (now U.S. Senator) Norm Coleman began, and after those debates, Ventura's share of the vote in the polls more than doubled to 21 percent. He was then able to obtain the resources necessary to run television commercials, and he ultimately won the contest with 37 percent of the vote. Had he not been allowed to debate, there is simply no way that Ventura could have won that election. As he himself said: "I was allowed to debate. I proved that you could go from 10 percent to 37 percent and win if you're allowed to debate. Rest assured, the two parties don't want to see that happen again."

In their current form, general-election presidential debates are elite-driven: the major-party candidates answer predetermined questions from a panel of elite journalists who typically talk only to themselves and their colleagues about the issues of the day. Walter Cronkite, a former panelist in presidential debates, has described this process as an "unconscionable fraud" designed to "sabotage the electoral process." Such a process, which serves to effectively insulate candidates from the electorate, has worked, as I have shown, to make it virtually impossible for independent candidates to reach the electorate and hence become viable candidates.

But, it is my judgment that, despite the CPD and its procedures, the whole nature of debates is changing, and the YouTube debate is but one example. Debates are becoming more than dialogues between elite journalists and candidates. Rather, they are evolving into dialogues between the electorate and candidates, a type of dialogue that we have only seen occasionally in presidential politics. It's no accident that the format that worked best for Ross Perot in 1992 was the town hall meeting, where George Bush was famously seen looking at his watch, wondering how much longer the debate would be. Indeed, the lesson I take from the YouTube debate is that we are moving inexorably toward a process in which voters will be able to engage in a back-and-forth exchange with the candidates online, through broadcast and cable media, and through town hall meetings. Debates will be a large, but not the only, part of that process.

Meanwhile, what will be the criteria of inclusion for an independent in the presidential debates? The Commission on Presidential Debates has used a 15 percent threshold in the polls to determine whether the candidate can participate. However, I think the YouTube debate and the related interactive dialogues strongly suggest that the model needs to be changed to a more inclusive two-step test: whether a majority of the electorate wants a particular candidate to participate and whether that candidate is on the ballot in enough states to have at least a theoretical chance of winning the election. This test will change the process from one controlled by the leaders of the two parties to one driven by the electorate itself. More often than not, it is the electorate's strong desire that third-party candidates participate, and this desire has been almost systematically frustrated.

The CNN/YouTube debate was heavily promoted, and justifiably anticipated by an electorate anxious to hear the candidates speak to the real issues. "It's the equivalent of the networks broadcasting the Kennedy and Nixon debate in 1960," said Kathleen Hall Jamieson, director of the Annenberg Public Policy Center at the University of Pennsylvania and co-author of *Presidential Debates: The Challenge of Creating an Informed Electorate.* "It's a new move for a new medium."

The questions chosen were mostly intelligent, graphic, and direct. A lesbian couple wondered whether the leading contenders would support same-sex marriage. The women hugged each other. Two brothers from Iowa wanted to know what was being done about Alzheimer's research. A young woman with breast cancer removed her wig and poignantly asked, "What would you as president do to make low-cost or free preventive medicine available for everybody in this country?"

When "Billiam," a snowman, asked a question about global warming, it undoubtedly elicited chuckles from viewers. (*The Wall Street Journal,* however, took it as seriously as the candidates did, later running a front-page profile of the two twenty-something brothers who produced it.) One questioner, concerned about the environment, asked the candidates to raise their hands in response to the query "Who arrived here on a private jet?" It's a question few journalists would ever think to ask.

CNN News anchor Anderson Cooper presided over the proceedings, generally staying out of the way.

To many viewers, the debate was a major event on the time line of American politics. To be sure, most of the eight candidates clung to their scripts, typically using the questions as jumping-off points to pontificate on their positions in press-release fashion. The politicians equivocated with great style and often replied without giving straight answers.

Most of the postgame analysts gave the experiment good reviews, generally applauding this new format. If anything, most critics said that the questions were better than the answers, which bordered on the bland. The *New York Times* headline perhaps best summarized the overall result: "Novel Debate Format, but the Same Old Candidates."

The highlight of the exchanges occurred when Barack Obama and Hillary Clinton sparred on the issue of whether a president should pledge to have an open dialogue with "rogue leaders." Barack Obama was pointed and clear: he would have no problem during his first year in office speaking with the heads of state of foreign governments who were deemed leaders of rogue nations. Clinton said she would not make a similar commitment, and ultimately branded this pledge as naïve. The important thing is that this critical difference between the candidates was made known to the voters, through a process that had never been used before.

The other major criticism of this new format was that it wasn't truly democratic because the organizers chose the questions, rather than the people who submitted them. The likelihood of your question being aired was roughly 1 in 77. Here's a novel idea: Why not hold an online runoff and let the people vote on the best video questions? Jeff Jarvis, a former television critic, said, "It's our democracy, not yours, CNN. There is a need for order, but not control."

But CNN ultimately disagreed. "It's dangerous," responded CNN executive producer David Bohrman. "With the anonymity of the Internet, you can cross the line. There's a small, good gatekeeper function we still need to play. This is the first time that online video gets a seat on the table to help elect a president, and we don't want to let it fall on its face."

But I have to side with Jarvis on this one. Certainly, a few ridiculous questions will sneak in, but so what? A candidate also has the option of whether to respond or not.

Despite the debate about who should be the ultimate organizer of a debate, we are firmly entrenched in the so-called "user-generated content revolution." David Colarusso, a high school physics teacher from Lexington, Massachusetts, created a page on his Community Counts website that allows users to vote "answer" or "ignore" for each video question. (YouTube doesn't rank the debate clips.) "Web 2.0 has the potential to actually compel candidates to be genuine," Colarusso told *Newsweek*. "If there are enough people saying, 'Hey, listen to this,' then it's in the politicians' best interest to answer."

With all its imperfections and rough edges, the CNN/YouTube debate was still historic. No matter what you think of the result, it marked the beginning of a dialogue that is more inherently democratic than what we've thus far seen. It's the breaking down of the barriers posed by institutional walls, but it's even more. It also breaks down the insulation and isolation of the candidates. It exposes their weaknesses and, hopefully, reveals their strengths. It changes the game by ensuring that a far wider range of issues become part of the national discussion. Most important, it gives new meaning to the term "participatory democracy," forces the candidates to confront the problems head-on, and enables us to improve the way we conduct politics in America. If this idea continues to evolve and become more refined, we as a people are all the better for it.

The Republicans went through a similar line of questioning in November, again with CNN and YouTube as the sponsors. Some speculate that the GOP has not embraced the format out of concern about the questioners in particular and the Internet in general. Mitt Romney dropped out of the debate originally scheduled for September 17, and Rudy Giuliani claimed a conflict with his campaign schedule. Debate organizers then moved to reschedule.

According to *The Wall Street Journal:* "Republican Internet consultants are sputtering with disbelief [about the Giuliani and Romney decisions]. 'With all of the challenges we're facing next year, the last thing we need to do is snub a medium that millions are embracing,' says Patrick Ruffini, a blogger and former Internet consultant for Giuliani.' "

Let's hope the debates continue to improve and disclose more about the candidates. In the primary season, in a field of eight, it's difficult to rank and grade the performances. But if I were pressed, I would say that the American public was the real winner. If the candidates fidgeted a bit more because they didn't know in advance what they were going to be asked, good. It shows that this is the kind of exchange that stimulates dialogue, disagreement, and solutions to our problems. It shows the American voters how a candidate behaves under pressure. We should demand nothing less from a potential leader of the free world.

So far, the numbers endorse the CNN format. Some 2.6 million viewers tuned in that Monday evening in July 2007; 407,000 were in the 18–34 age range, indicating that this type of debate attracts a younger audience. Every campaign season features an effort to court the youth vote. Using the tools of the Internet seems a perfect way to do this.

The bottom line, however, is this: The nature of the debates is changing, and it's all for the good. We're moving away from an elite model and moving toward a citizen-interactive model. The determining factor is no longer who the politicians want to see in the debate, but who the American people want to see in the debate. Future debates are going to benefit both the independent candidates and the voters.

Several debates took place months before the primaries even began. They featured a dozen or more hopefuls from both parties. If nothing else, they proved that presidential debates will be far more open, far more accessible than they ever have been. We're getting different kinds of debates; we have interactivity on websites. With websites such as Generation Engage, we're told we can create our own debates using free videos. *Got a question for the presidential candidates? Let the cameras roll and sent it in!*

To that end, the Huffington Post, Slate, and Yahoo! News have sponsored an Internet-based mashup with Charlie Rose interviewing the Democratic presidential candidates. This process allows voters to compare the candidates' positions on various issues so they can access answers to the questions they find most important. In the future there will be more unfiltered questions; these questions will promote less posturing, less evasion, fewer meandering answers. It's almost certainly just a matter of the technology continuing to evolve to allow more interaction.

What will this mean for a third-party or independent candidate?

It's difficult to believe that credible independents can be kept out of the discussions as the process is opened up to more citizen participation and hence inexorably becomes more inclusive. What happened to Anderson in 1980, what happened to Perot in 1996, and what happened to Nader in 2000 and 2004 simply cannot happen as easily now. We're just not going to have a traditional system of elite-driven debates anymore. We're seeing a blurring of the lines between regular journalists, the elite media, the pundits, the bloggers, and anyone else who thinks his or her opinion should be heard. In the summer of 2007, we saw a monumental breakthrough. Participatory debates are the wave of the future and broader participation will inevitably result.

The entire process is changing. So we are not going to get away this year with three debates, stylized formats, canned answers, and only two candidates. The debate world is changing, and everyone who tunes in will benefit. Everyone deserves to be heard. Even the conventional media outlets have discovered that they have to do more to engage their readers and viewers.

We'll see even more debates, different kinds of debates, especially interactive ones. I can imagine a citizen questioner and a candidate actually having a two- or three-minute give-and-take in front of a national audience, discussing an issue in detail. It's the equivalent of the boss walking the factory floor to find out the real concerns of the workers.

The Commission on Presidential Debates will have to revise its playbook. For example, I don't think the commission will be able to get away any longer with limiting eligibility to candidates who poll at least 15 percent. In the first few months of 2007, some candidates who participated in the primary debates were at or below 1 percent. The Commission on Presidential Debates is apparently acknowledging that times have changed. It recently named Elizabeth Wilner, the former NBC News political director, to study new media technologies as they relate to the debates. I have some optimism that she'll have a more enlightened and open-minded view of who should be included as the campaign season winds down.

One event of late 2006 may inspire another new presidential-debate format. The site was Cooper Union's Great Hall in New York City, the place in which Abraham Lincoln delivered a famous 7,700-word speech denouncing slavery in 1860. To mark that occasion, Newt Gingrich, the former House Speaker, agreed to debate former New York governor Mario Cuomo. They had a high-minded political debate about issues that mattered. The moderator was *Meet the Press* host Tim Russert, and the event was made available in real time on Gingrich's website.

Before the debate, Gingrich suggested that the Republican and Democratic presidential nominees meet nine times between Labor Day and election day in 2008 to debate for ninety minutes each night on a single topic—with a timekeeper but no rules. Gingrich argued that the sorry state of the nation's political discourse demanded it. "The gap between the challenges we face as a country and the trivializing of politics as *Entertainment Tonight* is so stunning," Gingrich said. "There's a substantial public interest in a dialogue and a bipartisan, solution-oriented approach. The country gets to watch two adults have a conversation. By the end, the candidates would be different people."

It was likely one of the few issues that he and Cuomo agreed on. When the ever-articulate Cuomo weighed in about the current debate format, he said, "Ninety seconds to answer [a specific and focused question] is designed largely to test glibness, memory, spontaneity, and theatricality. What you should be testing is the person's judgment, wisdom, experience. You don't get that by hiding the questions from him and seeing if you can catch him by surprise." Marvin Kalb, writing on the op-ed page of *The New York Times,* said that the "nine-by-90" idea would be a terrific boon for the voters. "[Gingrich] was hoping that these nine debates would force substance into the final phase of a campaign that is almost certain by that time to be exhausted by cynicism, sound bites and 24/7 drivel," Kalb wrote.

This idea of an extended debate is not new. This proposal grew out of an idea that hatched in 1991 within a study group Kalb led at Harvard. Back then, scholars, journalists, and politicians were trying to find ways to improve the political process. The conclusion was to have a series of nine debates on successive Sunday evenings, when the television viewing audience would be at its peak. Kalb's group suggested that the networks provide ninety minutes of evening or prime time between Labor Day and election day for conversations or debates with the major candidates in a studio without an audience. In his op-ed piece, Kalb recalled, "Substance was key, no frills. We also suggested that each event be limited to a single subject. (In the current context, one conversation would almost certainly be about Iraq.)" We can easily imagine other topics.

In the past, the League of Women Voters set the format and parameters of the presidential debates, brokering demands between the two major parties. Currently the Commission on Presidential Debates does so. Third-party candidates, as has been noted, have been effectively excluded unless they reached a minimum of poll support, around 15 percent.

Will it be difficult to decide which issues are the most compelling to the American voter? I don't think there will be much debate about that. Start with foreign policy, immigration, Social Security, health care, and so on.

I don't think any one person or commission or journalist-moderator should be the arbiter of which are the most important issues. If we can't agree, then let's put it to a simple online vote. We can use the Internet to put the question to the public and tally the results to find the nine most important topics.

Perhaps we will finally have moderators who know how to moderate, meaning how to really engage the candidates in a debate. Think of a good moderator as the competent referee in a boxing bout. He stays out of the way, keeps the fight clean, separates the clinches, and makes sure the fighters keep boxing.

Give Anderson Cooper some credit in the CNN/YouTube debate described earlier. (He was called a host, not a moderator, a careful distinction made by the organizers, I'm certain.) He often followed up and prodded the candidates to actually answer the questions asked. Unfortunately, the sparring looked more like a gym workout than a championship prizefight. Future debates of this kind should improve the quality of the output.

It drives me—and many other voters I talk to—to exasperation when I see what televised debates have become. Not since Richard Nixon and John Kennedy faced off have the candidates mixed it up and actually argued forcefully about the issues. The debates are antiseptic exercises in which candidates deftly duck questions by displaying an often dizzying capacity to memorize and recite their party's playbook.

Even the debates that were organized to encourage spontaneity and interaction between candidates and the audience have been seriously lacking. Consider the "Town Hall" debates in 2004, in which the candidates' handlers stipulated that the questions had to be submitted in advance. The possibility for intelligent follow-up questions depends solely on a probing moderator (who must be "approved" by the principals ahead of time). The notion of a direct answer to a question is no longer hoped for, let alone expected. And the multicandidate get-togethers early in the election cycle have been merely a repository for sound bites. It's difficult to be heard and to stand out.

"It's a failure of leadership not to provide thoughtful answers to meaningful questions," Dick Dadey of the nonpartisan Citizens Union told the New York *Daily News*. "Oftentimes it is simply because they don't want to be pinned down on specific issues, so they can change their positions later."

A commenter at the Ballot Access News blog, Felipe Maurer, posted the following: "What I think is sad is [the] fact that presidential debates are just the opposite. It seems to me that every presidential debate is about reiterating what has been said before during the campaign, and that presidential debates are not debates at all. A valid, and to me appropriate, definition of debate is: To engage in a formal discussion or argument. This definition is clearly what we do not have in the U.S., and I think that true presidential debates should be required of ALL candidates with all other candidates present. The sad thing is that I do not think that it will ever come to pass as long as we have a 2-party system (or an any number-party system)."

Maurer has a point, but at least in 2008 there appears to be an effort to change the nature of the process, in the near certainty that unless there is some change in the way debates are organized and in the criteria used to determine which candidates are actually included, the impact of the debates will be limited. Further, the ability of independent candidates to actually break through in the way that Ross Perot and Jesse Ventura did will be almost eliminated.

One idea has been to go beyond the Commission on Presidential Debates and create a broad-based, neutral commission that includes major party representatives, but also network executives, scholars, and representatives of the major political campaigns and other interest groups. John Anderson proposed creating a nonpartisan Corporation on Presidential Debates, modeled on the Corporation for Public Broadcasting, with a board composed of distinguished citizens.

More generally, the intent has been to break the stranglehold of the two major parties, and to involve a broader range of political activists and interests in organizing both the participants in and the structure of the debates. Also, the Center for Voting and Democracy, now known as FairVote, has organized a Citizens' Debate Commission (CDC) to sponsor the 2008 debates. The CDC has been endorsed by a wide array of voting rights organizations on both the left and the right and by dozens of newspapers. The CDC would use very different criteria to determine who would be included in the debates than the Commission on Presidential Debates uses.

The CDC would invite candidates to debate if they roughly meet the criteria of the two-part test outlined earlier: Candidates would be included if they are on enough state ballots to theoretically win in the Electoral College and if they either attain 5 percent in national polls or register a majority in national polls that asked the American people whom they would like to see in presidential debates. When a similar poll was done before the 2004 election, a majority did want Ralph Nader to participate in the debates but opposed participation by any of the other minor-party candidates.

The nature of the debate process is being altered as a result of the YouTube debate and technological innovation. Broadening the makeup and scope of the group organizing the presidential debates will almost certainly generate more innovative formats for these debates.

A number of ideas have been offered to go beyond the YouTube debate. One idea would be for the public to submit questions through online videos. The videos would then be viewed and rated by the public and the questions that receive the most positive response would be offered to the candidates. Alternatively, the candidates could participate in a debate carried by the broadcast or cable networks, or they could participate in one that takes place exclusively online, where candidates answer questions posed online with online video responses of their own that could be disseminated in a variety of ways. We could even have our first full-scale online debate in campaign 2008. In such a debate, the American public could push candidates to be more specific or to clarify their responses. As one commentator said, "Imagine the debate's host turning to one of the candidates and saying, 'Hold on, Senator. Three-quarters of the people watching right now on the Web have just said that they'd like you to go back to the question they just asked you, because they feel you didn't answer it at all.' "

This is certainly on the horizon, if it's not possible already. (It almost worked right away during the CNN/YouTube debate. You had to admire the moxie of a young man with a goatee named Chris from Oregon, who said, "Whassup?" and then went on to ask the group to "do something revolutionary and actually answer the questions posed to you.")

Another idea is to put the audience on the stage and allow them or the voters watching at home to send e-mails or text messages indicating follow-up questions and attempting to hold the candidates accountable. Yet another idea, which might be difficult to organize but which offers extraordinary opportunities, is to provide the candidates with laptops and hang a giant screen behind the stage. As the candidates speak, other candidates could instant-message their thoughts to create a scrolling commentary and critique. The moderator would seize on the most provocative comments and use them to drive the debate. For example, while Senator Clinton is discussing foreign policy, Senator Obama might raise questions about her views and vice versa. Thus, a real-time interactive discussion would occur without political spinmeisters attempting to "explain" their candidates' comments.

For an independent candidate to have a real chance to win the election, the traditional elite-driven process must change fundamentally. There are substantial signs, such as the YouTube debate, the creation of the CDC, and the efforts of the blogosphere, to suggest that changes are already happening. Indeed, there is an effort now to force the major candidates to go on the record supporting broader participation in the debate process.

Yet the debates are about the only time during the campaign season when candidates make a feeble attempt to rise above the fray, although their usual motive is to offend as few potential swing voters as possible. The choreography of today's debates makes one almost long for a Lincoln-Douglas marathon without a moderator and a dozen postgame analysts dissecting the give-and-take. In modern debates, it's almost impossible to call one candidate the winner. They all end in a draw. But that could well be changing.

Rock the Debates, a new organization, hopes to persuade a large number of people in Iowa and New Hampshire to repeatedly ask the major Republican and Democratic contenders if they are willing to participate in an inclusive general-election debate. The question will be whether those candidates would agree in advance to participate in a debate at which anyone who is on the ballot in enough states to win would be invited. In all U.S. history, there have never been more than seven such candidates in one election, including the major-party nominees.

Rock the Debates encourages viewers to get involved. This means that when a candidate comes to your city or town to campaign, you team up with another Rock the Debater to draft a question and film a video. The idea is to ensure that the YouTube model, or at least a form of it, carries through the season and that voters, and not just the beat reporters, are constantly putting the candidates to the test on the campaign trail.

The two leading Democratic candidates have generally bought into the principle behind Rock the Debates. They are on record as saying that if they are nominated, they will consider debating all their general-election opponents who are on the ballot in enough states to possibly win a majority in the Electoral College. However, neither Hillary Clinton nor Barack Obama has explicitly committed to the idea. Senator Clinton has said:

> Well I would certainly be open to doing it . . . I . . . you know, I
> might . . . there might be a couple of people that I would be a little

bit reluctant about, but, you know, I am generally open to that. You know in New York we have a lot of parties; we don't just have the Democratic and Republican Party, we have a lot of other parties. And, you, I believe in . . . in free and open debate. So I will certainly consider it. I'm not going to make a 100 percent commitment, because it's a hypothetical, and I try to stay away from hypotheticals. But I take your point and I think that it's a very important one that we need to get as many people involved as possible, and that means having a lot of opinions out there that people can respond to.

In response to the same question, Barack Obama said:

When you have a winner-take-all system, then what happens, it's very hard for third parties to get a foothold. Which is why we never really, even when guys like George Wallace did have a hearing, the worse thing when Ross Perot did have a hearing and had millions of dollars, it's still very hard for them to get leverage. But the general point, my general attitude is as many people get a hearing as possible. But what we'll hear from the networks is . . . look, it's nice, we're not just setting up a platform for a theoretical debate, we're choosing the next president. . . . I get your point and I'm sympathetic to it.

Bill Richardson is the only Democratic candidate for president to explicitly commit to allowing all candidates to participate in the debate process if he is the nominee.

On the Republican side, Mitt Romney refused to make an explicit commitment to debate all candidates on the ballot, saying he would defer to both the positions of the Commission on Presidential Debates and the networks, as well as his own assessment of the situation later in the 2008 election cycle. He did say that if New York City mayor Mike Bloomberg runs, he would have to be included in the presidential debates. Similarly, Sam Brownback, U.S. senator from Kansas, also refused to make a commitment, saying he would consider the proposition at a later date because of the number of third-party candidates who now could conceivably be on the ballot. Only former Arkansas governor Mike Huckabee and Colorado congressman Tom Tancredo, two dark horse candidates, explicitly agreed to include all presidential candidates who were on the ballot in enough states to theoretically be elected president in the general election debate process.

The endless debate, of course, leads to the seemingly endless campaign. Is this a good thing? Many press critics contend that there are too many candidates and too long a campaign season—an arduous and often tedious qualifying process that wears down voter interest. How long can people put up with the constant campaign? I have to disagree with the skeptics. I contend that the 2008 debating season will finally allow voters to truly understand the positions of the various contenders as long as there are formats put in place that encourage the broadest possible participation and ensure that the widest range of voices are heard. Given the very slow process of political reform (which I'll talk about in the final chapter), we must rely on getting the candidates to debate as much as possible in as many new and different formats as possible.

YouTube and CNN should be just the beginning. In the end, the new, longer campaign season (extended by the early primary dates) will drive the necessity for more debates.

The world of debating has changed in a significant and fundamental way. Interactivity will become the norm at some point, and we've already proven how effective it is in drawing out the candidates. Interactivity really matters, a continuous back-and-forth between voters and candidates. The elitists will resist, and perhaps they should. They're going to continue to complain that this kind of inclusion will confuse the issues and make the process more difficult. But it won't confuse the voters. Like campaigns themselves, debates will now be structured in a bottom-up fashion, and not the top-down that we've been accustomed to in the past. The citizenry has demanded it, as they have demanded the participation of credible independent candidates. The endemic problems we face with the functioning of our democracy are simply too great to allow the traditional system of elite-driven, carefully choreographed debates to continue to prevail.

9

Crafting an Electoral Strategy

I would like to see a businessman run for President who could run this country like a company. Then maybe we will see different and hopefully better changes made.

—Woman, 40, Ohio

If an Independent was elected President, it would be like having a mediator between the two parties instead of having a president who is on one party's side.

—Woman, 35, Washington

I ARGUE THAT THE CHALLENGES FACING THE COUNTRY ARE NOT ONLY greater than ever before, but that because of rising partisanship in Washington, these problems are more intractable than ever before. The problems themselves have significance for our well-being as a nation, and indeed for the entire world. These are not trivial challenges. The war on terror, immigration, health insurance and the 45 million people who are lacking it, are problems that go to the heart of who we are as a people and who we are as a society. Moreover, changes in technology have now made it more possible than ever to make that dissatisfaction known. Through the Internet and through the interactivity that I've described earlier in this work, we are better able to register our frustration, measure it, analyze it, and record it in ways that were never before possible. In short, the combination of historic voter dissatisfaction, paralyzing partisanship, and technological change is laying the groundwork for a viable third-party candidacy.

It's one thing, however, for the pieces to be put in place. Two larger questions must be asked: How does a third party win nationally? And who is the candidate with the best chance of winning a national election? There are no easy answers to these questions, because a viable third-party candidacy has few precedents in American politics. Nonetheless, a review of recent experience provides a possible road map for how an independent might win in November 2008.

CRAFTING AN ELECTORAL STRATEGY

The greatest challenge facing a third-party candidate is how to create a strategy that will lead to victory in November. Clearly, the success of any third-party candidacy will depend initially on the candidate's ability to mobilize millions of Americans on his or her behalf. As Ross Perot did to great effect in 1992, a third-party candidate in 2008 will have to tap into the growing and pervasive voter resentments toward the political system. The candidate will have to create immediate and positive name recognition, to raise or have available the money necessary, and to put together an organization rapidly.

The success of a third-party candidate will depend in large measure on the personality involved. It will take a special and unique candidate, like Perot, to convince enough Americans to break with the traditional two-party system, ignore party loyalty, and cast votes for a third alternative. However, even if a third party is able to raise the necessary funds and put together the necessary organization to get on the ballot in all fifty states, crafting a Electoral College strategy is crucial to its success. What might that strategy look like?

DRAWING THE ELECTORAL MAP

In 1992, 19 million Americans, or almost 19 percent of the electorate, cast their ballots for Texas billionaire Ross Perot. It was the best showing by a third-party candidate since Theodore Roosevelt in 1912. Exit polls showed that if Perot had had a legitimate shot at winning, the numbers might have been even higher and exceeded one-third of the vote. I believe that had he not temporarily dropped out of the race in July and had he run his campaign differently, he would have had a chance at winning the White House in 1992.

Probably the untold story of Perot was that Mark Penn, my former business partner, had devised an absolutely brilliant plan with two California consultants, Arnold Ford and Bill Butcher, to galvanize the Perot constituency. Ford and Butcher were responsible for assembling the first authentic citizen-based grassroots movement in American politics, California's Proposition 13 to limit property taxation, and had developed a similar plan for Perot—a plan that, sadly, was never implemented. In early 1992, Mark and I had gone out to lunch with some Colombian clients, and when we came back to the office, we had an urgent message to call Ford and Butcher. We did, and they asked us if we wanted to do a strategic benchmark poll for Perot as a means of developing a strategy. As I was deeply involved in a number of Democratic campaigns at the time, I demurred, but Mark took the assignment. He did a brilliant piece of research that showed a number of things that proved to be prescient.

First, Penn found that for Perot, who had just announced his willingness to run for president if the American people wanted him to run and demonstrated their support by getting him on the ballot in all fifty states, there was enormous potential to win in 1992. This potential grew largely out of dissatisfaction with the two-party political system, a lack of enthusiasm for the likely nominees of the two major parties, and frustration with the budget deficit. Doing some very sophisticated modeling, the type of modeling that rarely took place in American politics, Penn discovered that Perot could likely get in excess of 40 percent of the national vote with a platform based on attacks against the political system combined with a strong economic-growth message.

Penn, Ford, and Butcher, drawing from their findings, suggested that Perot hold a giant nominating convention, one that would be different from those held by the major parties. They suggested that the convention take place in the Rose Bowl on July 4, 1992, and that it bring together the hundreds of thousands of volunteers who had been organized across the country as well as new volunteers, to formally begin his bid for the White House. California was a critically important state to Perot, which was another benefit to having the event at the Rose Bowl, and his speech would get a great deal of attention on the Fourth of July. Such a convention would have been an enormous rallying point for the campaign; it would have focused attention on Perot's message. It would have galvanized the electorate in a way that is now impossible to quantify, and in retrospect I believe that it could well have catapulted Perot into a strong, indeed dominant, position. But Perot ultimately disregarded this suggestion as well as most others that came from his advisers.

Despite this missed opportunity, the polls in June 1992 clearly lend credence to Penn's analysis. A little-remembered compilation of polls from that month, published in the *National Journal*'s *Hotline,* indicated that Perot might win enough electoral votes to gain the presidency. These numbers were based on the results of state polls from forty-two states; they gave 284 electoral votes to Perot, 158 to President Bush, and only 16 to the eventual 1992 winner, Bill Clinton. Three states were tied and eight states, plus the District of Columbia, weren't even included.

Such strong early results are not unusual among third-party

candidates. In 1980, another year of strong voter dissatisfaction, John Anderson polled as high as 24 percent at one point during the campaign. Even George Wallace cracked 21 percent in 1968.

But unlike in the 1992 race, when Perot led the field for a time, no poll ever found Wallace or Anderson ahead. Had Perot's candidacy not been sunk by his own early reluctance to spend money, his paranoia and mistrust of the political system (and, in particular, his political consultants), it isn't unreasonable to suggest that he could have won.

The poll results shown in Figure 13 provide compelling evidence of Perot's extraordinary political rise in the spring of 1992 and the viability of his candidacy. The data showed that as of June 1992, Perot was ahead in twenty-one states with 284 electoral votes.

Some may argue that it's impossible to extrapolate from Perot's performance to today's political realities. That's true, to an extent, but keep in mind that people are even angrier today than

FIGURE 13. **State of the Race: Perot's Support in June 1992**

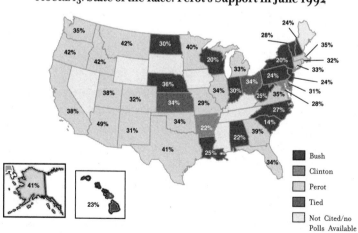

Source: *Hotline*

they were then. I've been around the country, I have looked at the polls, I've talked to voters; I have seen and heard it firsthand. I believe that with the right candidate and the right campaign, 55, 60, or even 65 percent of the American people who have told pollsters they would consider voting for an independent could be mobilized quickly to actively consider that very possibility.

Moreover, Perot's support was hardly based on a "none of the above" mentality. A fascinating poll taken just before the election showed that 45 percent of those supporting Perot did so because of his stance on the issues, 24 percent liked his leadership qualities, and only 19 percent supported Perot because they didn't "like the other candidates." A plurality of voters thought that of the three candidates Perot would do the best job of handling the economy. Other polls gave Perot the advantage on dealing with taxes. Yet another indicated that a majority of voters (51%) thought Perot would do a better job on the deficit.

For all his faults—and they were many—Perot was able to tap into a growing sense of voter disenchantment in 1992. Today, with voter disenchantment at least as high, it's not hard to imagine that a candidate who aggressively seeks the White House as a credible independent could do better. If Perot, with all his personality quirks and the absence of a political résumé, could still score close to 20 percent of the vote in a national election, a better qualified candidate could easily better that total.

For these reasons, any discussion of an effective electoral strategy for a third-party candidate must begin with Perot's 1992 campaign and, in particular, an examination of the places in which Perot did the best in 1992—states in which he was able to exceed 20 percent of the vote. This provides a baseline of states where realistically a third-party candidate could do well enough to win. Don't forget, in a three-way race for the White House, a viable third-party candidate only needs to garner 34 percent of the vote in a state to win that state's electoral votes.

In 1992, Perot did his best in Maine, where he won 30 percent of the vote, narrowly edging out President Bush. In general, the Northeast was fertile ground for Perot. He cracked 20 percent in New Hampshire, Vermont, Connecticut, Rhode Island, and Massachusetts. Representative John Anderson had done well in the region in 1980. Although he won just about 6 percent of the overall vote, Anderson broke 10 percent in six northeastern states—a feat he achieved in only three other states.

Perot's highest support came in the Far West, where he won between 20 and 25 percent of the vote in California, Washington, Wyoming, Idaho, Alaska, Oregon, Utah (where he surpassed Clinton), Colorado, Arizona, and Nevada. He also scored between one-fifth and one-quarter of the vote in the Plains states, including Nebraska, Oklahoma, Kansas, Missouri, North Dakota, and South Dakota, and the Upper Midwest, Minnesota and Wisconsin. The challenge for Perot and for any third-party candidate comes in the South, the Midwest, the border states of the old Confederacy, and the lower Northeast (New York, Pennsylvania, and New Jersey). This is where a successful third-party candidate will have to significantly improve on Perot's showing in order to win the 2008 election.

Even here, however, there is some reason for hope for a third-party candidate. While the South was not a strong region for Perot, the June poll numbers showed him leading in Florida, Georgia, Virginia, and his home state of Texas. In Illinois he was ahead, and in Ohio he was tied for the lead. While it's hard to imagine a third-party candidate winning those states today, Perot's strong numbers suggest that such a candidate might, at the very least, be competitive with the two major candidates, forcing them to spend money in places where they would naturally expect to face limited risk. Perot's final vote tally and his performance in spring and summer polling indicated the wide geographic swath of his appeal.

FIGURE 14. **Perot Support in the 1992 General Election**

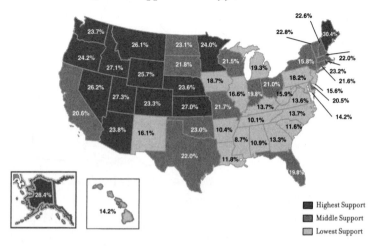

Source: *Hotline*

Besides the Perot voters, one must look at those places where third-party or centrist candidates have scored success in non-presidential elections. A popular notion in American politics posits that third-party candidates rarely if ever win, but a look at the political landscape over the past fifteen years shows that, in certain circumstances, centrist-minded third-party candidates have been able to overcome the institutional power of the two-party system and win elections.

GOVERNORS

After president, governor is the most senior executive position in American democracy. In many respects, a governor has more of an impact on Americans' lives than even the president. Repeatedly, in recent years, we have seen voters cast ballots for third-party and reform-minded candidates.

In 1998, in Minnesota, voters supported the long-shot bid of wrestler-turned-politician Jesse Ventura. Running on an out-sider message of "Don't vote for politics as usual" and positioning himself as a fiscally conservative, socially liberal candidate, Ven-tura won 37 percent of the vote, just enough to put him over the top in a tight three-way race.

In 1994, Maine (which had given Perot his largest share of the 1992 vote) elected Angus King, an independent, as governor. King had no political experience, having worked as a commenta-tor on a local Maine PBS channel and as a businessman. Again, King's opponents were no slouches: current U.S. senator Susan Collins and two-term former governor Joseph Brennan. King won with 35 percent of the vote—in a race with eight independent candidates.*

King's idea, that government simply wasn't working, had a particular impact in Maine, where a Republican governor, John McKernan, and a Democratic legislature had been gridlocked. The state government had actually shut down for two weeks in 1991, and the economy was performing badly. "The voters were looking for someone with new solutions," says Douglas Hodgkin, a profes-sor of political science at Bates College, in Lewiston, Maine.

King had solutions on every page of *Making a Difference,* his 130-page campaign treatise. But he also had the outsider's privi-lege of asking obvious questions. "I tell groups: 'The bad news is, I don't know the rules. The good news is, I don't know the rules,' " King said. "It's a fresh-eyes approach. I can look at things and say: 'Why are we doing it this way?' "† In 1998, King ran for re-election and won with an impressive 59 percent of the vote.

In more recent years, independent-minded gubernatorial candidates have continued to score strong results. Although he

---

*"Who Is Paying for Gubernatorial Elections in Maine?" Maine Citizen Leadership Fund, 1994. Via opensecrets.org.
†John Powers, "Declaration of Independence: Rebel-Turned-Entrepreneur and Now Gov-ernor of Maine, Angus King Defines a New Breed of Politician," *Boston Globe,* June 11, 1995.

ran as a Republican, Governor Arnold Schwarzenegger is exactly the kind of centrist, postpartisan candidate who seems most capable of doing well on a national stage. After his initial victory in the recall election against then governor Gray Davis, Schwarzenegger eschewed bipartisan compromise. To his initial detriment, when asked if he would negotiate with Democrats in the state senate, he said that he saw no reason to "talk with losers."* He also called Democratic politicians "girlie men," a reference to a famous *Saturday Night Live* skit.

While his approach had some initial, limited success, traditional political partisanship was not working and the governor faced some initial setbacks. In a November 2005 special election, he tried to pass four ballot measures, all of which went down to resounding defeat.

During his reelection campaign, Schwarzenegger began to tack toward the middle, looking for areas of compromise with Democrats and tackling issues that had broad appeal, like climate change and energy efficiency. He began positioning himself as a doer, a governor inclined to compromise and one pursuing independent-minded, centrist political strategies. While still a Republican, Schwarzenegger was certainly out of step with the direction of the national Republican Party. During his campaign, he spent as much time extolling his bipartisan virtues as he did his Republican ones. Californians responded, and in the 2006 election, which nationally featured an overwhelming Democratic victory, Schwarzenegger polled 56 percent of the vote.

In New York City, Mayor Mike Bloomberg has taken a similar approach. Although he ran for the mayoralty as a Republican, his positions lay pretty firmly in the Democratic Party tradition, from his position on gun control to those on abortion and gay marriage. While he went through the motions of being a Republi-

*Audrey Kim, "California Dreaming," *Harvard Political Review Online,* May 28, 2007.

can, such as raising money for President Bush, he rarely, if ever, engaged in partisan attacks on Democrats, instead maintaining his image as a technocrat and doer. The result was a narrow victory in 2001 and a huge reelection victory in 2005, in a city in which registered Democrats outnumber registered Republicans by a significant margin.

In Texas, as I discussed earlier, during the 2006 gubernatorial election, two political independents, "Kinky" Friedman and state comptroller Carole Keeton "Grandma" Strayhorn, shocked the state's political world by scoring about 40 percent of the vote in a multiparty race. In Oklahoma in 1994, a disaffected Democratic congressman, Well Watkins, got close to a quarter of the vote as an independent. And in 2002, also in Oklahoma, a Republican businessman, Gary Richardson, got 14 percent in the gubernatorial election as an independent.

Connecticut is another state in which independent candidates have fared quite well and voters have shown an inclination to ignore long-held party affiliation. Joe Lieberman won reelection to the Senate as an independent in 2006 after losing in the Democratic primary to Ned Lamont. Lowell Weicker left the Republican Party and won the governor's race in 1990. Weicker launched a third-party bid after concluding that the Republicans had moved too far to the right. Weicker had lost his Senate seat to Lieberman in 1988, in part because conservatives abandoned him. William F. Buckley had run a "Weicker Watch" in the *National Review* and organized a "Buckleys for Lieberman" group to funnel money toward the Democrat.* Launching a bid for governor under the "Connecticut Party" banner, Weicker gained 40 percent of the vote, beating Republican John G. Rowland (who won 37 percent) and Democrat Bruce A. Morrison (who won 21 percent).†

---

*Maralee Schwartz, "Buckleys for Lieberman, Believe It or Not," *Washington Post*, August 16, 1988.
†Kirk Johnson, "Choice of Governor; Old Face Brings Change to 'Land of Steady Habits,' " *New York Times*, November 8, 1990.

Granted, a third-party candidate could not win the presidency on the strength of Minnesota, Maine, Connecticut, Texas, and California alone. These examples suggest, however, that, if presented with a centrist, independent-minded candidate focused more on solving problems than casting stones, Americans are willing to give that candidate a chance and will be receptive to his or her overtures. These elections occurred in places that run the political gamut—from conservative Texas to more liberal California, New York City, and Maine. Minnesota has consistently elected politicians from across the political spectrum—for example, the ultra-liberal Paul Wellstone and the right-wing conservative Rod Grams. These results demonstrate, I believe, that enough voters out there, if given a real choice, would elect a third-party candidate who promises genuine change.

In a recent poll that I conducted in 2006 for the Aspen Institute, an extraordinary 95 percent of Americans agreed that "we need to find common solutions to our problems that both Republicans and Democrats agree with." Three out of four reported that they think the American Dream is "somewhat broken," and more than 60 percent said that they believed they are "not living" the American Dream. These numbers suggest a true crisis of confidence in America—one that an independent can exploit.

PLAYING THE KINGMAKER

Obviously, crafting an electoral strategy and achieving it are two very different things. Certainly, the odds are against a third-party candidacy winning the White House. It would be foolish, however, to assume that such a candidate couldn't, at the very least, have a significant and far-reaching impact. History often has demonstrated that third-party candidates can have a fundamental impact on major policy debates.

In 1912, Theodore Roosevelt's candidacy under the Bull

Moose banner helped give rise to the progressive reforms that would come during the presidency of Woodrow Wilson. His split from the Republican Party also helped enshrine the GOP as the party of small-government conservatism.

Although he lost in 1968, George Wallace highly influenced (many would argue negatively) the national debate on civil rights. His antigovernment rhetoric would serve as a template for a generation of conservative politicians, led initially in 1972 by Richard Nixon with his so-called "silent majority." In 1980, John Anderson scored only 6 percent of the vote, but his third-party run raised the profile of such critical national issues as fiscal restraint, environmentalism, Social Security reform, and energy independence. As a former aide to Anderson argues, "He did get Americans thinking about a realistic Third Way that married social compassion to fiscal responsibility. You could argue that Gary Hart and Clinton followed in his wake."[*]

I have a clear and unambiguous sense that the most important person in the 1996 election was Ross Perot, who in 1995 shaped and prefaced the outcome of the election the next year. It is very simple: But for the balanced-budget initiative of Bill Clinton, which our team fought for and won in 1995, I don't think the president would have been reelected. Moreover, I believe that it was because of Perot's candidacy that the drive for fiscal discipline, cutting spending, and bringing government within its means stimulated what Bill Clinton accomplished in '95 and ran on the next year. The balanced-budget initiative, on which Clinton beat the Republicans, was fundamentally a repackaging of the Perot message for the mainstream. It was a nonpartisan, values-based, centrist message; it spoke to fiscal discipline first, which was the essence of Perot, but it also reached to protect our values, the environment, Medicare, Medicaid, and our education sys-

[*]William McKenzie, "Take Chance to Turn Debate," *Hartford Courant*, July 3, 2007.

tem. The success that Bill Clinton had in 1995 in my judgment won the '96 election, moved Clinton to the political center, and positioned him as a mainstream, nonpartisan American politician who did what was right and stood up for American values. Thus, the work we did that was so successful for Clinton in repositioning the Democratic Party was really a result of the Perot candidacy. Perot deserves credit for raising the profile of the budget issue and for placing it front and center in American politics. I believe a third-party candidate in 2008 could have the same effect.

Unlike other political systems, American democracy is a winner-take-all system. While compromise has always been at the heart of our political system, it's not essential. With control of both houses of Congress and the presidency, one political party can drive its political agenda with minimal interference. If it can produce a filibuster-proof majority, as Franklin Roosevelt and Lyndon Johnson had, it can operate with virtual impunity. But it doesn't necessarily have to be that way in 2008.

In America, we've never countenanced the notion of a coalition government, but a third-party candidate could force such a situation, positioning him- or herself as a kingmaker. There are a number of ways to have such an effect. Clearly, there is the Perot 1992 approach of focusing national attention on one or two critical issues. But third-party candidates can also have a different, more immediate effect. If no candidate receives 270 electoral votes, an independent candidate could use his or her electoral votes either to force attention to specific issues or to bargain with each of the two major parties for a role in the government.

But before we consider how candidates might bargain and negotiate in the Electoral College, it is important to note that there have already been significant moves to change the Electoral College system itself. Most of those changes would almost certainly benefit a third-party candidate. For example, there have been all sorts of discussions about proportional allocation of electoral votes, and two states, Maine and Nebraska, have taken concrete steps to do just that in the past. My belief is that the fairest system is the one that Maryland is now implementing, whereby the winner of the country's popular vote wins Maryland's electoral votes, regardless of the state's actual tally. This move by Maryland is an inexorable step toward the elimination of the Electoral College, which I believe is a healthy step for our democracy. Instead of having a thirteen-state contest where candidates only compete in states that are up for grabs, as happened in 2004, candidates would have to run a real national campaign.

But the more fundamental issue is that where we have a proportional division of electoral votes—as we now have in Nebraska, Maine, and potentially even California, should a 2008 ballot initiative be approved—we are now seeing a populist desire for alternatives that empower people rather than effectively disenfranchising them. There is an increasing desire in the electorate for a system that does not reduce or eliminate the influence of voters in some states, that instead makes every vote count and gives every voter an opportunity to make his or her voice heard. Even if one dislikes the California initiative (as many Democrats do because it is most likely a Republican tactic to get the GOP some delegates in a reliably blue state), one has to understand that it does reflect the frustrations of an electorate that wants to have an impact and be part of the presidential election process. And, as former congressman Martin Frost has written, if the California system of allocating electoral votes by congressional district is adopted there and elsewhere, "this would make it easier for third and fourth party candidates to win some Electoral votes and thus increase the possibility that no one would win a majority of Electoral votes on Election Day."

Even with the current sclerotic Electoral College system,

there are a myriad of ways an independent could influence the ultimate choice of president, even without any change in how electors are selected.

DUELING IT OUT IN THE ELECTORAL COLLEGE

There are two ways an independent could make a difference in the Electoral College. First, if an independent candidate wins a plurality of electoral votes and not a majority, he or she could simply bargain with one of the two major candidates, combining their electoral votes and effectively creating a coalition government. It's not outside the realm of possibility that an independent candidate who receives between 200 and 220 electoral votes could make a deal where cabinet positions would be shared and policy positions melded to create an independent-Democratic government or an independent-Republican government with a mixture of the major platforms of the two parties. While this may not sound realistic at first, if the Republican candidate finishes third to strong independent and Democratic candidates, the Republicans would have to choose: either support the independent for president and effectively share power or be out of power totally. Specifically, they could be part of an independent-Republican administration and have significant cabinet positions, or they could be consigned to the minority and potentially be in opposition in Washington for an indefinite period of time. In such a situation, the independent could actually become president despite winning less than a majority of the popular or Electoral College vote.

Another very possible option was posited by Patrick Healy in *The New York Times.* If an independent candidate were to win a few major states (like California and New York) and receive 60 or 70 electoral votes, he or she could prevent either of the two major parties from receiving the needed 270 votes. In the last two presidential elections, the Electoral College winner, George W. Bush, won 271 and 286 electoral votes, respectively. In the 2000 election, an independent candidate would have only needed to win one state for neither major-party candidate to win a majority. In 2004, an independent who carried Ohio, New York, or Florida would have had the same result on the election. Considering the nation's sharp red/blue divide, it would not be difficult for such a situation to occur. Again, the independent could bargain with one of the parties to create a coalition in which the independent would be a junior partner. As in the first scenario, there would be a sharing of cabinet positions and a melding of philosophies. Either scenario could result in America's first-ever coalition, power-sharing government, with the independent as either the junior or the senior partner in the coalition.

In a deadlocked election, if no side was willing to offer concessions, the Electoral College could meet and choose a consensus pick that was not one of the original three candidates. Since electors are under no obligation to vote for any specific candidate—even the ones on the ballot—any number of scenarios or candidates could emerge from the Electoral College. While all of these scenarios seem remote now, each one could theoretically occur. For those who say all of this is improbable, my response would be that the circumstances that decided the 2000 election after thirty-six days of wrangling and court challenges seemed improbable right up to the time that they actually occurred.

THROWN INTO THE HOUSE

If no coalition government was worked out in the Electoral College and the election was thrown into the House of Representatives, similar bargaining could take place there. In such a scenario at present, a Democratic candidate would likely win, since the party controls twenty-six state delegations, and to win a candidate would need a majority of the fifty state delegations, each of which would vote as a unit. However, if the independent candidate had done extremely well in the election, he or she could call on the delegations from states where he or she had done very well to vote for him or her so that the will of their constituents was reflected in the final vote. If the state delegations did not comply, the threat, however vague, would be that the independent would actively oppose any congressional delegation in the next election whose vote didn't reflect the will of its electorate.

Alternatively, an independent candidate who did well in the popular vote could seek a commitment from the delegations who vote for either of the major-party candidates that they will entreat their choice to agree to implement all, or at least part, of the independent's platform. The bottom line is that the possibilities for national horse trading over the White House and the terms, platform, and makeup of the next government are limitless.

It is possible that if the election is deadlocked in the House, a coalition between two of the three candidates might emerge. If the deadlock isn't resolved, the election might be thrown to the Senate, where the vice president is selected, and he or she would become the president if no president is selected in the House. This individual could be a Democrat, a Republican, or an independent. And what if the Senate is unable to come to an agreement? Well, then prepare yourself for President Pelosi—the Speaker of the House, who is next in the line of succession after the president and vice president, would enter the Oval Office.

Nevertheless, the electors or House delegates are under no formal legal obligation to vote according to the mandate of each state's electorate. Thus, House delegates could simply follow party lines and vote for the Democratic candidate even if the independent candidate won the most (but not a majority of) votes in the Electoral College. However, if the independent candidate receives that many electoral votes, this will likely be seen as a strong enough public mandate to prevent either body from going against the will of the public.

At the very least, as we saw in the elections of 1948 and 1968, an independent candidate could try to use his or her electoral votes or vote total to focus national attention on his or her issues. In 1948 and 1968, Strom Thurmond and George Wallace ran for the presidency for precisely this reason. If a candidate wins enough electoral votes to throw the election results into doubt, the winning candidate must at least pay deference to the individual and his views. Of course, Thurmond's and Wallace's platforms were narrow and negative, focusing on race and the desire of southern whites to protect their position. These days, the agenda of an independent is likely to be much more broad-minded and to address issues that concern voters of varying philosophies. An independent could initially mount an independent campaign and, if it did not appear to be heading toward victory, could drop out at some point before election day and make an alliance with one of the major-party candidates. Such a move could win support for policy initiatives supported by the independent and land key positions in the next administration for the independent and his or her supporters.

In short, an independent candidate could run for reasons other than just winning the White House. He or she could play the role of the kingmaker, forcing lawmakers to enact specific policies backed by the candidate's supporters, regardless of how many votes or states he ultimately prevails in. While it is not too much to expect a third-party candidate to upend the political system and win a national election, it's also very likely that a third-party candidate could in a multitude of ways impact the nation's ultimate choice of the president, or at least the national agenda. If a third-party candidate ran on a platform of bipartisanship demanding that the two parties work together to develop long-term solutions to the problems of terrorism, energy independence, and immigration, that would be as significant and important a contribution as anyone could make to the 2008 presidential election campaign.

THE CANDIDATE

There are a number of people who are obvious candidates, but the one thing that we have seen in America, from Anderson, Perot, Howard Dean, and now Barack Obama and Fred Thompson, is that credible candidates become known very quickly. They can raise money and build support using the media and the Internet in ways we never thought possible. Of course, this is easier if the candidate has strong name recognition and credibility as a national figure, but in this world that is only helpful, not essential. The challenges and costs in making Americans aware of a third-party candidate in a national race are enormous.

Clearly, money is a key consideration for a third-party candidate. In some ways it is easier to raise money than ever before, but of course a candidate with deep pockets starts in a much more advantageous position.

A strong third-party candidate would need to espouse a strong centrist political message, encompassing fiscal conservatism, a commonsense approach to immigration, moderation on social issues, and a firm, internationalist approach to fighting the war on terror. It's important that the candidate be willing to take on tough issues and put all policy choices on the table, to eschew the politically correct and to make it clear that he or she was going to put aside short-term political considerations. I think the candidate who has the will to consider cutting entitlement programs, as well as to raise taxes in order to balance the budget, to protect the environment, and to reduce dependence on foreign oil, will obtain more support for taking these positions, even if they challenge the conventional wisdom about what is effective in political campaigning. My sense is that a candidate who demonstrates that willingness to take on the established orthodoxy could quickly develop strong national support.

The most obvious name for the head of a third-party ticket would be that of New York mayor Mike Bloomberg. Bloomberg has deep pockets: he has spent over $150 million on two races for mayor. He has reasonably strong name recognition, both as a hugely successful entrepreneur and as a very effective and popular mayor of New York. He has an almost perfectly centrist, pragmatic, nonpartisan political identity. Having switched party identification from Democrat to Republican in order to run for mayor in 2001, he announced in the summer of 2007 that he was leaving the Republican Party and registering as an independent—a move that sparked speculation he might run for president.

I have spoken to Bloomberg personally about the '08 race and he made clear to me as he had to others that, as of the summer and fall of 2007, he was not planning a presidential campaign—though he dangled enough hints that it was clear his denial was not absolute and unequivocal. Like many Americans, he feels deeply disturbed by the level of partisan rancor in Washington and the breakdown of the political system, and if he came to believe he had a real chance to win and hence could fundamentally change the political system, I think he would seriously reconsider.

Ruminating on the mood of the public on Mark Green's Air America radio talk show in 2007, Bloomberg tantalizingly opened the door to a 2008 examination of a candidacy:

> *You have to have a situation where the public is not satisfied with the choices, wants a third alternative. Where the public says there's too much partisanship, let's go to somebody who's not affiliated with either of the two major parties. It's a daunting task be-*

*cause we do have a two-party system, and a certain percentage of
the public will always vote in the party they're registered in. But
we have had third-party candidates before. I think Ross Perot did
the best in terms of getting 19 percent of the vote. Whether or not the
country really wants that, it's not easy to say today. But after the
selection process plays out with both the Republican and Democratic parties, we'll see. The public may feel that they don't have
any choice.*

Sources directly familiar with Bloomberg's thinking say that
he will indeed reconsider his options once both parties' nominees become clear.

Kevin Sheekey, Bloomberg's top political aide, said that he
would wait until March 5, after the Texas primary, when the nominees from the two major parties presumably will have been chosen, to assess the situation once and for all. His self-described
"Sheekey Master Plan" would use two criteria in making a recom-
mendation to Bloomberg. First, are 70 percent of the American
people convinced that the country is off on the wrong track, and
second, do 40 percent of the American people view the presump-
tive nominees of the major parties unfavorably?

Sheekey said that Bloomberg could well run if the two parties put forward nominees who play to their bases but ignore the
center. As for Bloomberg changing his mind, Sheekey saw little
problem with that. "If there's a reason for you to run and there's
a constituency that's calling for you, and you have real ideas,
then people will support you." And Bloomberg's quasi-denials
of interest so far? "I have not heard anyone run around talking
about Barack Obama saying, 'He swore he wasn't going to run.'
Because no one cares. They care about what he's going to do for
the country."

Former Democratic senator Sam Nunn of Georgia and Nebraska senator Chuck Hagel have acknowledged talking with

Bloomberg about an independent challenge to the major parties. Nunn has summarized his conversations with Bloomberg as follows:

> *We've had conversations about frustration with the fact that the process is flawed. I've told him . . . it may be time for some serious people to look at what I call a time-out and having people of good faith in the Democratic and Republican parties to come together and address the issues that the parties don't seem to want to address.*

Nunn said that for himself it was a "possibility and not a probability" he would run for president as an independent or as part of a bipartisan ticket. He rationalized his possible candidacy by citing the "fiasco" in Iraq, the out-of-control federal budget, U.S. energy policy, and a presidential campaign that has not taken on the real issues facing the country in a serious way. "I am frustrated with the fact that my children and grandchildren are not going to have the kind of future they should be having," Nunn said.

Hagel has gone a step further, saying that it requires a leader like Bloomberg to address partisan gridlock and the failure of the major parties to address the intractable problems facing the U.S. like the war in Iraq, the subprime lending crisis, and the immigration issue. "A guy like Bloomberg could have deep credibility as a candidate," Hagel has said. "He's a fresh face and a proven leader. It could be he'd release a dynamic that would be an answer for many people."

For his part, Bloomberg in June 2007 delivered a major speech in Los Angeles at a conference appropriately titled Ceasefire! Bridging the Political Divide. That conference did a good job of spelling out his concerns while also laying the potential framework of a third-party political platform. He said:

America, the most wonderful country in the world, is at a cross-roads. The politics of partisanship and the resulting inaction and excuses have paralyzed decision-making, primarily at the federal level, and the big issues of the day are not being addressed—leaving our future in jeopardy. We can accept this, or we can say "Enough is enough!" and together build a bright future for our country.

I believe we can turn around our country's current, wrong-headed course, if we start basing our actions on ideas, shared values, and a commitment to solve problems without regard for party.

We do not have to accept the tired debate between the left and right, between Democrats and Republicans, between Congress and the White House. We can and we must declare a ceasefire—and move America forward.

While a ceasefire is essential, it must also be followed by change. Real change—not the word, but the deed. Not slogans, but a fundamentally different way of behaving—one built on cooperation and collaboration. And it is needed now—because more than ever, Washington is sinking into a swamp of dysfunction. No matter who's in charge, sadly, today, partisanship is king.

It's become a contest to one-up the other side and to score points for the next election. Decisions in D.C. these days are more political and less issue-based than ever before, and the consequences have been disastrous.

This is paralyzing our government—and it's leading our elected officials to push all the big, long-term problems onto future generations: health care, Social Security, budget deficits, global warming, immigration, you name it.

There aren't many Americans who would disagree with this assessment—and with Bloomberg's image as a centrist and non-partisan leader, he could certainly run a campaign based on these principles. If he believed that by running it would advance change, he might well consider throwing his hat in the ring.

Beyond political independents such as Bloomberg, some disaffected Democrats and Republicans could mount a campaign, among them Senator Chuck Hagel, who has been virtually ostracized from the Republican Party because of his position on the Iraq War. Hagel is a political conservative but he has put forward a nuanced, internationalist position on foreign policy, a position that I believe would find broad public support. In addition, Hagel has advocated campaign finance reform and the need to clean up the political system. Unfortunately, these positions have alienated him from his own party. In a May 2007 appearance on CBS's *Face the Nation*, Hagel spoke of the political distance that has grown between him and the Republican Party:

> *I've been a Republican all my life. I voted for the Republican ticket in 1968 when I was in Vietnam. I'm not happy with the Republican Party today. It has drifted from the party of Eisenhower, of Goldwater, of Reagan. The party that I joined, it isn't the same party. It's not. It's been hijacked by a group of single-minded almost isolationists . . . power-projectors.*

Moreover, Hagel initially refused to rule out a third-party run:

> *I think a credible third party would be good for the system. It would force both parties that have been hijacked by the extremes of their two parties—and I think we would want something like that. I would hope this country has some options like that. I think it shakes the system up. The system needs to be shaken up. . . . We need some new fresh independent ideas to lead this country forward.*

However, by the fall of 2007, Hagel had closed the door on a run for the White House in 2008, saying he did not plan to be a candidate for national office. He has, however, met privately with Bloomberg, and even positively commented on CBS about a

Bloomberg-Hagel ticket in 2008: "It's a great country to think about a New York boy and a Nebraska boy to be teamed up leading this nation." A ticket of Bloomberg and Hagel would have enormous appeal for disaffected Democrats and independents as well as moderate Republicans. It would provide a broad geographic appeal—an urban and a rural candidate—and both politicians' strengths would complement each other nicely. A Bloomberg-Hagel combination, under a Unity08 banner, would be powerful.

Others who might be considered include prominent businesspeople such as Bill Gates, Steve Jobs, and Jack Welch, and even former newscaster Tom Brokaw or current CNN commentator Lou Dobbs. At first glance it may not seem politically likely that any of them would run, but after the polling I have done and with thirty years of experience, I can say that a credible businessman, running on a platform of change, would be able to instantly gain political credibility and political support. All of these individuals have deep pockets and strong name recognition and are respected as effective businesspeople or communicators. With dissatisfaction as great as it is, a smart, centrist businessman could emerge as the head of a ticket. If it worked for Perot in 1992, it could work again in 2008. Each of these individuals is also worthy of a vice presidential nod and could bring a decidedly nonpolitical angle to the ticket. Think about what would happen if someone like former Federal Reserve chairman Alan Greenspan said he was available for one term. If such a candidate ran with someone with international experience, like former UN ambassador Bill Richardson or former general Wesley Clark, such a ticket could be instantly credible.

Other politicians merit consideration. In the summer of 2007, John McCain's campaign seemed dead in the water, largely because he abandoned the Straight Talk Express that won him such accolades (and independent support) in 2000. It may seem far-fetched, but he could potentially decide to revive his campaign by working with Unity08 for its nomination. Rudy Giuliani could also seek such a path if denied the GOP nomination because of his moderate positions. Even Al Gore could throw his hat into the independent ring—an easier route to the White House than the minefield of the Democratic nomination process.

When pollster Scott Rasmussen posited in 2006 that a third-party candidate would run on a strong immigration/protect-the-borders platform, the independent moved into a virtual tie with an unnamed Democratic and Republican opponent. When Rasmussen substituted a strong pro-life position for immigration, the third-party candidate still got about 15 percent of the vote—a figure very similar (18%) to what CNN pollsters obtained when they repeated the same question in early November. These results have as much to do, in my judgment, with the theoretical possibility of a third-party candidate emerging and advocating clear and unambiguous policy positions as they do with the specific policy positions being advocated. When Michael Bloomberg merely announced in June 2007 that he was disaffiliating from the Republican Party and becoming an independent—all the while insisting that he had no plans to launch a bid for the White House—his support for president roughly doubled: the next poll showed him shooting up close to 20 percent, depending on the precise matchup, as you will see in Figure 15.

Moreover, at a time when 27 percent of the electorate told Rasmussen in a separate survey that they might conceivably support Bloomberg, his support increased significantly if voters were presented with a situation where he had a hypothetical chance to win. Rasmussen explained to his sample that there could well be a three-way race for president between Clinton, Giuliani, and Bloomberg, with the Republican having little chance of winning. After giving those circumstances, Rasmussen asked his sample how they would then vote, and their responses showed Bloomberg moving ahead of Senator Clinton. When Ras-

FIGURE 15. **Support for Bloomberg for President, June 2007**

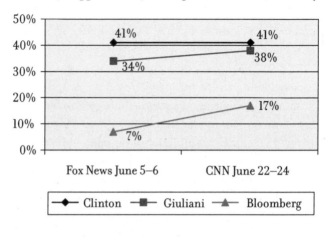

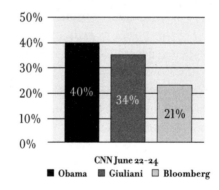

mussen postulated that there could be a three-way race where the Democratic candidate, Senator Clinton, had little chance of winning, Bloomberg moved into a statistical tie with Republican Rudy Giuliani.

Of course, this does not necessarily mean that Bloomberg, or any independent candidate, will see his level of support increase in this way. Indeed, after the media frenzy surrounding his announcement died down, Bloomberg's support quickly fell back to

TABLE 4. **Suppose the Republican/Democratic Candidate Could Not Win. Who Would You Vote For?**

	BLOOMBERG	**CLINTON**	**GIULIANI/ DON'T KNOW**
If Republican couldn't win	46%	37%	17%
	BLOOMBERG	**GIULIANI**	**CLINTON/ DON'T KNOW**
If Democrat couldn't win	34%	35%	31%

about 10 percent, the level at which it has remained through November 2007, since his disaffiliation from the Republican Party in June of that year. But a look at some additional data collected by Rasmussen Reports in the summer of 2007, as well as a look back at history, suggests that what happened, however briefly, with Mike Bloomberg's poll support following his disaffiliation from the Republican Party, could well happen in 2008 should a credible independent enter the race.

Rasmussen's data shows that there is now a broad base of potential support for an independent candidate in 2008. Almost one-third of American voters (31%) said they had already voted for a third-party candidate for president in the past and close to three-fifths (57%) said it would be good for America to have a viable third-party candidate in 2008.

Far and away the strongest possible independent candidate, according to Rasmussen, is former general and former secretary of state Colin Powell, who polled at or above 30 percent in trial heats against Hillary Clinton and Rudy Giuliani and against Rudy Giuliani and Barack Obama. As Figure 16 shows, Powell ran second behind Senator Clinton, trailing by only 9 percent, and edging out Rudy Giuliani. Against Barack Obama, Powell did even

FIGURE 16. Colin Powell as an Independent

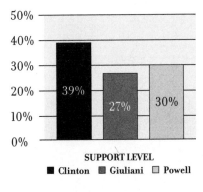

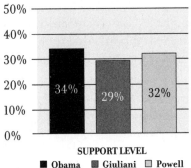

Source: *Rasmussen Reports, September 2007*

better, finishing in a statistical tie with the Illinois senator and ahead of the former New York mayor.

When Rasmussen turned to other prospective independent candidates, John McCain, Al Gore, and Tom Brokaw each garnered more than 15 percent running against the then Democratic front-runner, Hillary Clinton, and the then Republican front-runner, Rudy Giuliani. Bill Gates garnered 15 percent in a three-way matchup, comedian Stephen Colbert 13 percent, and former Federal Reserve chairman Alan Greenspan also got 10 percent, as did comedian Jon Stewart and talk-show host Oprah Winfrey.

FIGURE 17. 2008 Additional Presidential Election Matchups

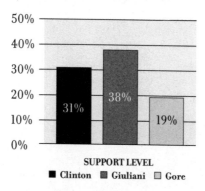

SUPPORT LEVEL
■ Clinton ■ Giuliani □ Gore

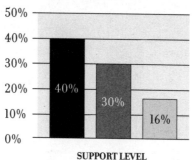

SUPPORT LEVEL
■ Clinton ■ Giuliani □ McCain

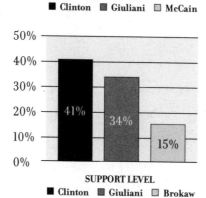

SUPPORT LEVEL
■ Clinton ■ Giuliani □ Brokaw

FIGURE 17. Continued

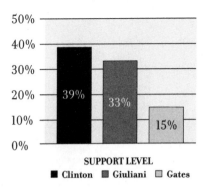

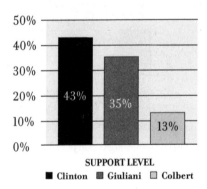

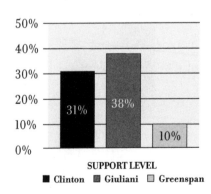

FIGURE 17. Continued

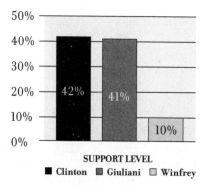

SUPPORT LEVEL
■ Clinton   ■ Giuliani   □ Winfrey

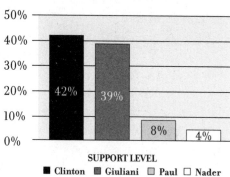

SUPPORT LEVEL
■ Clinton   ■ Giuliani   ■ Paul   □ Nader

Source: *Rasmussen Reports, September 2007*

Thus, before a campaign was even launched, a well-known independent was at least within striking distance of the leading Democratic and Republican candidates.

Finally, when Ron Paul and Ralph Nader were added to trial heats against Giuliani and Clinton, they both were in single digits. In such a hypothetical contest, Clinton led Giuliani by 3 percent, with Paul getting 8 percent and Nader 4 percent. A more in-depth look at the data shows that Brokaw, for example, does best with the voters I have already described as the RAMs—that is, independents and self-described moderates of middle age and lower or

TABLE 5. **Support for President**

	UNNAMED DEMOCRAT	UNNAMED REPUBLICAN	INDEPENDENT/NON-DEMOCRAT OR NON-REPUBLICAN
Answer Volunteered	41%	24%	15%

middle income. He also ran strongest with those who had the lowest level of trust in government and those who felt both the Democrats and Republicans were not serious about addressing the real problems facing America. Colbert, by contrast, did best with voters under thirty, winning 28 percent of their support and getting more than a million to register support on his Facebook page in just over a week. The *Washington Post*/Kaiser/Harvard University poll similarly showed that about 15 percent of the electorate volunteered that they support an unnamed independent against an unnamed Democratic or Republican candidate for president.

Further, the Rasmussen survey showed that more than half of the electorate (53%) said both parties were not serious about addressing the real problems facing the country and only slightly more than one-quarter (27%) disagreed. Accordingly, it's hard not to be surprised that a large segment of the electorate perceived that they had substantial differences with the major-party candidates on the issues and suggested that these differences could lead them to support a third-party candidate. A solid majority of Rasmussen's sample of likely voters indicated that they

TABLE 6. **How Likely You Will Disagree with Both Democratic and Republican Candidates on the Following Issues**

	GOVERNMENT ETHICS	IMMIGRATION	HEALTH CARE	IRAQ	ECONOMY
Expect to Disagree with Both Candidates on Issues	61%	59%	54%	53%	53%

TABLE 7. **If You Disagreed with Both the Republican and Democratic Candidates, Would You Consider Voting for a Third-Party Candidate Who Shared Your Views on That Issue?**

Would Consider Supporting an Independent Candidate Who Agreed with You on Each Issue	GOVERNMENT ETHICS	HEALTH CARE	IRAQ	ECONOMY	IMMIGRATION
	52%	51%	51%	48%	43%

expected to disagree with both the Democratic and Republican presidential candidates on virtually all of the major issues facing the country. Well in excess of two-fifths of the electorate indicated—in keeping with earlier findings—that they would consider voting for a third-party candidate who shared their views on the issues on which they differed substantially with the major-party candidates.

The implications of these findings for the 2008 election seem clear and straightforward. The landscape is fertile for an independent candidate to pick up support quickly from disaffected voters. My best guess is that an independent candidate who is credible could quickly garner one-fifth to one-quarter of the vote after his or her announcement of candidacy. At that point, the electorate would most certainly take a hard-headed look at the third-party alternative, and if they find the candidacy compelling, there is every reason to believe that the support will continue to grow. Indeed, it is the argument of this book that because of the challenges confronting us, and the tools available to mobilize a disaffected and angry electorate, a third-party candidate actually has a real chance to successfully contest the 2008 election.

I am virtually certain that when confronted with these possibilities, each of the aforementioned politicians and businessmen would angrily and steadfastly deny any interest or desire to run.

My point is only to suggest that a credible third force or independent, running on a nonpartisan, results-oriented platform, could quickly produce levels of support at or perhaps even above what Ross Perot garnered in the spring and summer of 1992. It's not that far-fetched, and if Unity08 or an independent is able to produce a credible alternative, the levels of support might be greater than anyone currently deems possible. The system is more open now than at any other time in history. The unhappiness with the political system is at a record high, while the technology is in place to allow a third-party candidate to make his voice heard in a credible way and to get on the ballot. At the very least, an independent running could fundamentally impact the policy agenda and change for the better the politics of our country and the politics of Washington.

10

The New Language of Politics

*In the new century, we need to reassess our thinking and learn to
do things differently and better. The government is failing us and
we need to get those old-time professional politicians who can't
think out of the box out of there before the country ends up in ruins.*

—WOMAN, 40, Ohio

WHETHER A THIRD-PARTY CANDIDATE CHOOSES TO RUN IN 2008 OR
not, an independent political movement has the potential to
change the way all political leaders think, talk, and act on the national stage. A centrist, independent-minded agenda can come
from either of the political parties or from an outsider—but it
must come, because Americans demand it. We are facing a crisis
of confidence in America. Politics as usual is no longer accept-
able. Difficult and uncomfortable questions need to be asked and
addressed. Another presidential election that features harsh
partisanship and rhetorical games, rather than increased calls
for bipartisan compromise and national unity, will be a disaster
for the country.

Americans want change. Any candidate considering a run for
the White House in 2008 can read the polls: they tell a vivid tale of

disillusionment with the state of the country and the political system. More Americans think the country is on the wrong track than at any time in recent history. A plurality believes that their children will be worse off in the future; only a third think their children will be better off than we are today.* The optimism that once came to define America is slowly but surely disappearing.

As for the nation's political leaders, President Bush is experiencing the most sustained period of presidential unpopularity in American political history. His approval numbers have not cracked 50 percent since January 2005, and over the past year close to two-thirds of the American people have consistently registered disapproval of his job performance. Even the newly elected Democratic Congress receives abysmal grades from the American people, and an August Gallup poll shows congressional approval at historic lows. What's worse, Americans increasingly don't trust their elected leaders. A recent Battleground Poll found that 71 percent of Americans believe their congressional representative is putting partisan politics ahead of the national interest.† This speaks to the genuine disillusionment with the political system that so many Americans feel. Moreover, a *USA Today/* Gallup poll in early November 2007 found that voters across the board were much more likely to say they were inclined to vote against each and every presidential candidate than they were to support them—indirectly representing dissatisfaction with the process more so than with the candidates themselves.

The ongoing breakdown of party loyalty is as inexorable as it is clear. The 2008 election could well be an election as transformational as 1932 was for the Democrats—it ushered in the New Deal—and as 1980 was for the Republicans in setting the stage for the "Reagan revolution." But I believe the 2008 election will not be a realigning election like those of 1932 and 1980. Rather, the stage is set for it to be a *de*-aligning election, in which the ties of

*Dan Balz, "Pessimism Nation," The Trail blog, WashingtonPost.com, July 27, 2007.
†Ibid.

the electorate to the major parties are further frayed, allowing for the emergence of a third-party candidate. Polling that my former firm has conducted, as well as polling done by Stanley Greenberg for the Democracy Corps, suggests that we are not entering a new era of liberal, activist government. In truth, voters are becoming increasingly cynical and demonstrate a record level of skepticism about the government's ability to effect positive change, and increasingly convinced that government is a negative force that only wastes the taxpayers' money.

Scott Rasmussen's polling cited in chapter 9 showed that a majority of the electorate expected that they would disagree with the major party candidates on *all* the major issues facing the country—the war in Iraq, immigration, the economy, and so on. Former Republican National Committee chairman Ken Mehlman underscores this basic point by arguing that both the Republicans and the Democrats are exhausted and would benefit from new ideas to address the challenges we face today:

> *If you look back over the last few decades, an era of politics has run its course. Both parties achieved some of their highest goals. Democrats got civil rights, women's rights, the New Deal, and recognition of the need for a cleaner environment. Republicans got the defeat of the Soviet Union, less violent crime, lower tax rates, and welfare reform. The public agrees on this. So the issues now become: How do you deal with the terrorist threat? How do you deal with the retirement of the Baby Boomers? How do you deliver health care with people changing jobs? How do you make sure America retains its economic strength with the rise of China and India? How that plays out is something we don't know yet.*

I believe the candidate that most ably reflects and responds to this overarching sense of disenchantment and exhaustion will reap the greatest rewards in November 2008, whether that candidate is running on the Democratic, the Republican, or an independent ticket. Moreover, I think all Americans will benefit from a third-party bid because the bid can only help restore faith in our national institutions and create a broader sense of national unity in tackling America's most pressing challenges—a quality this nation has lacked for at least the past seven years.

In many respects, a third-party candidate would be best positioned to gain from the present crisis of confidence with American government and with a broad array of American institutions: beholden to no interest group, able to voice a nonpartisan message and breathe some fresh air into the political scene. All these attributes would give a third-party candidate unique opportunities not only to be competitive in an election campaign, but also to raise new and important issues and embolden a new generation of political activists.

The respondents to the independent interviews I conducted in September 2007 put it simply and directly.

"A third-party candidate would clearly encourage more independent thought where the issues are not so predictable and where everything now is black and white."

"Almost invariably, we would have more progress made on issues that have traditionally been stalled."

"A third-party campaign would provide a more logical viewpoint with better ideas on how to actually solve problems rather than creating more."

But of course, the strength of the two-party system suggests that a smart Democrat or Republican can tap into these concerns as well—the way they always have, by co-opting the issues that third-party candidates bring to the national agenda. Already, we are seeing evidence that individuals in both parties are getting the message and are reflecting on the campaign trail Americans' desire for a nonpartisan approach to politics. As Ronald Brownstein has recently put it in his new book, *The Second Civil War: How Extreme Partisanship Has Paralyzed Washington and Polarized America,* "The overriding message for both parties from the Bush attempt to profit from polarization is that there remains no way to achieve lasting political power in a nation as diverse as America without assembling a broad coalition that locks arms to produce meaningful progress against the country's problems."

THE NEW LANGUAGE OF POLITICS

The frustration many Americans feel about the political system is already finding voice in campaigns. The candidacy of Barack Obama, a first-term U.S. senator from Illinois, provides a good example of how the new language of political compromise can reap dividends. When he announced his intention to seek the presidency on February 10, 2007, he sounded the postpartisan themes that have come to define his candidacy:

> *What stopped us from meeting these challenges is not the absence of sound policies and sensible plans. What's stopped us is the failure of leadership, the smallness of our politics—the ease with which we're distracted by the petty and trivial, our chronic avoidance of tough decisions, our preference for scoring cheap political points instead of rolling up our sleeves and building a working consensus to tackle big problems . . .*
>
> *This campaign has to be about reclaiming the meaning of citizenship, restoring our sense of common purpose, and realizing that few obstacles can withstand the power of millions of voices calling for change.*

This is exactly the kind of language that Americans want to hear from their elected leaders. Obama's extraordinary fundraising record, as well as his unquestioned position as a front-runner in the Democratic primary, derives in large measure from his message of conciliation, his pledge to bring a new spirit of effective governance to Washington, and, above all, his inspirational message of national renewal.

Barack Obama's problem is that although he is speaking to the agenda of the Restless and Anxious Moderates, the RAMs are a small percentage of the Democratic primary electorate. It is the activists who vote in primary elections by and large, and they have an ideologically driven agenda, fueled by the left and by the blogosphere. It may be very hard for somebody with Obama's undeniable personal appeal to succeed in a primary where his not fully articulated agenda is subsumed by his biography. Still, Obama has seen his support grow substantially in Iowa, New Hampshire, and South Carolina based on an appeal that emphasizes rejection of partisanship and voters' desire for a new kind of politics that encourages national unity.

Unfortunately, Obama's inspirational message has been missing from the Democratic Party for the past several election cycles. That such an untested leader should excite such enthusiasm—in the fundraising period for the second quarter of 2007, Obama's campaign received contributions from 250,000 people, an extraordinary number of small donors—indicates the potency of a nonpartisan political message in 2008, even if his rhetoric and approach are not, in fact, ideally suited to a Democratic primary audience.

One interesting element of Obama's candidacy is that he regularly eschews obvious attacks against the Bush administration. Speaking to Democratic primary voters, Obama would certainly garner some benefit from attacking the deeply unpopular president. But he rarely mentions the president's name. This is smart politics for a general election but not as wise for a primary contest when the incumbent president of the opposing party is deeply unpopular and literally invites attacks.

Nevertheless, the Republican pollster Frank Luntz pointed

out, "In every focus group I have conducted in the last two years, I've heard the same conclusion again and again: 'Don't tell us what George W. Bush did wrong. Tell us what you will do right. Don't talk about the past. Tell us about the future.' " Not every Democrat is getting this message, but Obama is one candidate who certainly seems to understand that the broader electorate, if not Democratic primary voters, hanker for less partisanship and an inclusive appeal.

Obama is not the only one preaching bipartisanship. Senator Hillary Rodham Clinton, long a divisive figure for millions of Americans, has used her campaign speeches to call intensively for greater cooperation and less partisanship. Like many Democrats, though, she has become increasingly critical of President Bush, both as a means of focusing attention on the ultimate target in campaign 2008 and also serving to blur distinctions among the various candidates on the Democratic side who are trying to make her record the focus of their attention. This is undoubtedly a smart strategy on her part but does entail some risks. She has wisely taken steps to underscore that she too is a conciliator, and her health-care proposal, unveiled in September 2007, emphasized a significant degree of cooperation among employers, insurance companies, and ordinary Americans. Consequently, she won support from many who opposed her original health-care plan when it was unveiled in 1993.

In a Labor Day weekend speech in New Hampshire, Senator Clinton sought to speak to both her primary and her general election constituencies, all the while maintaining that she can and has produced real change. She spoke passionately of the need to build compromise and consensus to achieve real successes such as FDR's creation of Social Security and LBJ's passage of the Voting Rights Act. She spoke of seeking "common ground, as a necessary precursor to achieving real results." But her conclusion deftly made it clear that she would never compromise on what she really believed. "Ultimately, to bring change, you have to know when to stand your ground and when to find common ground. You need to know when to stick to principles and fight, and know when to make principled compromises." She has also spoken of the need for a "postpartisan" political agenda as a means of better bridging the gap between the left and the right. It is a delicate balancing act, one that will almost certainly persist through the whole nominating and general election process.

In maintaining that delicate balance, she will no doubt be assisted by her husband, former president Bill Clinton, who instinctively knows how and when to reach the Restless and Anxious Moderates. In a little-reported presentation at the Aspen Ideas Festival in July 2007, the former president took pains to find ways to praise President Bush for some of his foreign policy initiatives—on disease control and North Korea, for example—demonstrating that he understands the importance of finding common ground with the political opposition.

Unlike most politicians in Washington, Senator Clinton has come to understand the importance of bipartisanship. She saw the effectiveness of it when I was advising President Clinton during the 1995 budget battle with Congress. She saw the pitfalls of failing to reach across party lines during the health-care debate in the early 1990s. In 1998, she saw her husband run a progress-over-partisanship campaign during the height of the Lewinsky scandal that brought surprising Democratic gains in that year's midterm elections—even though historically the sixth year of a two-term incumbent brings losses for the party in power at 1600 Pennsylvania Avenue.

Lastly, during her first Senate campaign in 2000, with the help of my former partner, Mark Penn, she organized listening tours and ran a consensus-based campaign that sought to dispel the image of her as negative and divisive (an image more reflective of outmoded stereotypes and her opponents' distaste for her than of her own personality). Of course, it worked extremely well, softening her image and providing a test model for a presidential run in 2008.

Today, she continues to sound bipartisan notes. At a January 2007 speech at the New America Foundation she said, "I don't think Americans are looking for some kind of group-hug bipartisanship—I think they're looking for leaders who can get back to reality-based policy-making. . . . The answer is not that we're going to get rid of partisanship—as long as there are human beings jousting for influence and position, they're going to take all kinds of opposing, partisan stances. . . . But it does mean that we can be smarter about how to narrow the differences between partisan ideas, and try to eliminate the partisan gamesmanship."*

During her tenure as New York's junior senator, Clinton has repeatedly reached across the political aisle to work with some of the most conservative members of the Republican Party on issues ranging from health care, the military, and veterans' issues to education and curtailing violence in video games.

As the Democratic nomination battle has taken form, however, she has of necessity had to try to sound more partisan in order to curry favor with liberal Democratic primary voters, many of whom look skeptically at some of the positions she has staked out on foreign policy, especially what they perceive as her vote to authorize the Iraq War (a characterization she disputes).

This is one of the unfortunate elements of the nominating process in American politics. Candidates are pushed to be more partisan and divisive in order to win their party's nomination. If Senator Clinton is forced to move too far to the left and become overly partisan during the primary—something she has so far deftly managed to avoid doing—it will create difficulties for her

*Patrick Healy, "Senator Clinton: Compromise 'Not a Dirty Word,' " The Caucus blog, nytimes.com, January 31, 2007.

candidacy in the general election should she emerge as her party's standard-bearer.

Should she win the Democratic nomination, I fully expect that her record of working with Republicans in crafting effective public policy solutions will be one of the cornerstones of her campaign. It's the kind of record of bipartisanship that the American people have made clear they are seeking from their elected leaders.

Indeed, Hillary Clinton has the appeal, rhetoric, and positions of someone who would be a compelling third-party candidate. However, she is still commonly seen through an ideological lens, despite her efforts to mute partisan perceptions of her candidacy. She understands better than many the difficulties of running for office and, indeed, of governing as a narrow partisan Democrat, and will almost certainly take significant steps to alter this perception.

In New York, Mayor Mike Bloomberg has focused on results over partisan fervor or acrimony, and he has reaped the political rewards. His centrist, can-do attitude toward government has met with strong support both in New York and around the country. As his adviser Mitchell Moss noted, "People looked up and realized that Bloomberg had made government work in New York."*

Like few politicians in America today, Bloomberg seems to understand and empathize with the voters' frustration. As he recently said in a *New York* magazine profile: "The public wants government to address long-term issues: who's going to pay for spiraling health care costs? Or solve our foreign-oil dependency problem? Or pay for retirement costs or take on the environmental issues? . . . Politicians talk about fiscal responsibility, and yet they're building up this unconscionable deficit, which means your children and

*John Heilemann, "His American Dream," *New York*, December 11, 2006.

grandchildren are going to have to pay for the services the elected officials are promising to the public today. It's a disgrace."* Those are the words of someone who understands what the electorate is seeking as we approach the November 2008 election.

"They're frozen," California governor Arnold Schwarzenegger said of Congress. "They can't do anything in Washington because it's Democrats against Republicans, Republicans against Democrats, rather than, 'Let us solve the problems of this country.' "† In a speech in June 2007, Schwarzenegger laid out his philosophy for change:

> *For America to continue thriving as a great democracy that can inspire the rest of the world we need new ways of doing the people's business. All of our most deeply held dreams and aspirations require us to build on our common bonds rather than keep resorting to the tired battle cries of partisan politics that divides and demoralizes us. We need new methods of breaking through the political gridlock to make progress on issues that people care deeply about, issues like health care, climate change, immigration, border security, education, the economy, public safety, and the list goes on and on and on.*

With an approach like this, it's hardly surprising that in 2006, a year when Democrats won handily across the country, Schwarzenegger easily won reelection in one of the bluest states in America.

The new language of consensus is also bringing success in less high-profile locales. Ohio governor Ted Strickland is an interest-

---

*John Heilemann, "His American Dream," *New York*, December 11, 2006.
†Joe Mathews, "Pumped Up," *Los Angeles Times*, November 4, 2006.

ing example of how positively voters are responding to politicians who leave the divisive rhetoric aside. *Washington Post* columnist E. J. Dionne jokingly called Strickland "Mr. Consensus" because of his nonpartisan approach to governing. Even though Strickland stands decidedly on the left of the political spectrum, he remains immensely popular in a state that Republicans have historically dominated—and where George Bush won in both 2000 and 2004.

According to Strickland, "people are desperately wanting to believe that political leaders understand them and that they are trying to deal with their day-to-day lives."* Strickland's success goes to show that if political leaders, Democrat or Republican, make a concerted effort to work across the political aisle and reach out both to supporters and to those less inclined to vote for them, voters will respond.

In May 2007, Strickland had the highest approval rating (68%) in the history of the Ohio Poll, conducted by the University of Cincinnati. When asked to explain the extraordinary results, Strickland shared the glory, attributing the numbers "to bipartisan cooperation with the Republican majority General Assembly on higher education financing, economic development, and lowering property taxes for senior citizens."[†]

A later poll, in July 2007, showed that *half of all Republicans* approved of Strickland's performance. In a state that was as polarized and divided as Ohio was in the 2004 election, such numbers are extraordinary and demonstrate the success of post-partisan governance.[‡]

---

*E. J. Dionne, "Mr. Consensus Makes Inroads," *Washington Post,* July 24, 2007.
[†]Joshua Boak, "Strickland Approval Rating Highest in Ohio Poll," *Toledo Blade,* May 15, 2007.
[‡]"Strickland Approval Rating Explodes; Voinovich Has Sub-50 Approval Rating," Buckeye State Blog, July 13, 2007, http://www.buckeyestateblog.com/strickland_approval_rating _explodes_voinovich_has_sub_50_approval_rating.

Former Virginia governor Mark Warner is another example of a successful elected official who won broad bipartisan support by advocating initially controversial policy positions that addressed the long-term systemic problems of the state. His tax reform package, which involved some increases in taxes as well as limits on spending, won significant Republican support when it was enacted. Warner rejected short-term fixes to Virginia's economic problems and instead made tough decisions, which, when enacted, won broad public support.

He left office with an 80 percent approval rating and briefly mounted a presidential campaign, which he abandoned in mid-2007. He is now running for retiring senator John Warner's seat on an explicit program of conciliation and bipartisanship.

"The American people want a big ask," Warner told me. "I am betting they will respond well to politicians who ask them to make big sacrifices for the national interest. My campaign is based on that logic, and I will not be afraid to reach across the aisle to embrace Republican-originated plans if we can develop long-term solutions to the problems of terrorism, controlling entitlements, and providing for the long-term well-being of America."

Unfortunately and unwisely, the Republican side of the aisle has voiced fewer calls for bipartisanship and reconciliation. This may explain the fundraising challenges confronting the party and the party's dwindling support among the electorate. Republican candidates are catering to the conservative wing of the party by harshly attacking Democrats. It may be an effective strategy in the GOP primaries, but in a general election such an approach could prove to be a liability. The kind of divisive politics that brought electoral success to George W. Bush is fast becoming an anachronism.

Rudy Giuliani would be an ideal third-party candidate. He had a nonpartisan centrist appeal as mayor of New York and won broad bipartisan support for his efforts on and after 9/11. He also supported an inclusive social policy and has significant across-the-board support as a result. As a Republican presidential candidate, however, he has had to move decisively to the right on immigration, gun control, abortion, and gay rights, all the while positioning himself as the strongest in the war on terror. This has weakened his appeal as a general election candidate, while it makes him more palatable to the Republican base.

John McCain's candidacy provides a cautionary tale about the dangers of trying to appeal to the base. When he was "driving" the Straight Talk Express in 2000, McCain enjoyed broad support among independent voters and even some moderate Democrats. For a brief time at the beginning of the Bush administration, McCain worked with both Democrats and Republicans. More-over, he continued to play up his postpartisan, solution-based approach to politics, which resulted in strong approval numbers, especially among independent voters.

McCain's independent streak was considered so strong that he was seriously considered as a possible running mate for John Kerry in 2004.

That was then. As soon as his rhetoric took on a more partisan tone and he became more closely identified with President Bush's unpopular policies, particularly his policies on Iraq, McCain's support among moderates plummeted. His tactical decision to seek out the support of the evangelical wing of the Republican Party ended up having a negative effect on his presidential aspirations. Evangelicals were not persuaded and moderates were deeply offended. Moreover, his support of immigration reform cost him significantly among conservatives and mitigated whatever benefit he might have garnered from supporting the president on Iraq.

Clearly, McCain suffered a grievous blow to his candidacy by taking the positions he did. But it could well have been different. He could have said,

> *"I'm going to run as an independent. I'm going to tell the truth about the war, about immigration and about tax cuts. I'm going to tell you that I thought the tax cuts were wrong, that the war has to be fought but we need more troops, and that we need a balanced policy on immigration."*

Had he done that, I believe he would have been in far better shape than he is today. I believe the Restless and Anxious Moderates could well have rallied to him, and I believe he would have commanded a high level of national support. He certainly would have been true to his worldview.

All things considered, an Obama-McCain or McCain-Obama third-party ticket would be at least as credible as any pairing the Democrats or Republicans could mount.

A CHANGING POLICY APPROACH

As the threat of a centrist revolt becomes more evident, I expect the nature of political campaigns and language of politics to change along with it. As more Americans express disillusionment with the political system, mainstream politicians will need a new way to communicate with these fed-up voters.

The examples I've cited above are simply the tip of the iceberg. Along with employing the new language of bipartisanship, a number of political leaders are taking steps to address the growing insecurity of voters. Nearly all of the Democratic nominees for president have devised detailed health-care plans stressing policies that expand coverage to the nearly 47 million Americans who lack health insurance. In addition, a number of the candidates have been talking about broadening access to college, lending a helping hand to workers who lose their jobs because of global trade, and allowing the government to negotiate directly with pharmaceutical companies in order to lower the cost of drugs for Medicare recipients.

Democratic politicians have stated clearly that these steps are being taken in order to restore confidence in America's governing institutions and the capability of government to solve pressing national challenges. According to House Speaker Nancy Pelosi, "I don't think we'll be able to do trade agreements, immigration reforms or any of these other kinds of reforms until we present a positive, aggressive economic agenda to the American people—until they know where we stand, now and in the future."*

Of course, such populist measures can have negative consequences. These are already being seen in a Democratic pullback from free-trade agreements and increasingly class-warfare-oriented rhetoric, especially from those who advocate higher taxes on the wealthy and in particular on private-equity firms and hedge funds. This is not to say these aren't defensible positions. Not only are they defensible, they may very well be good public policy. But a focus on inequality and nakedly populist rhetoric is not what Americans will be looking for in 2008. Polls that I have taken provide ample evidence: 74 percent want government to pursue policies that grow the economy for everybody, while only 26 percent believe government should pursue policies that redistribute wealth from the richest to the middle class and the poorest.

These policy discussions demonstrate that even if an independent doesn't win, a centrist third-party candidacy articulating a nonpopulist inclusive economic agenda could change the entire context of the 2008 race. Already we are seeing Democrats wisely focusing their attention on the pocketbook issues that could shape the next election. This emphasis demonstrates that a third-party campaign, or even the threat of one, could very well change the nature of American politics from one of bitter parti-

*Robin Toner, "A New Populism Spurs Democrats on the Economy," *New York Times,* July 16, 2007.

sanship and red-versus-blue demagoguery to one focused on finding solutions to America's problems.

A HISTORY OF THIRD-PARTY INFLUENCE

As has already been shown, when it comes to major national issues such as slavery, Prohibition, the federal deficit, and civil rights, as well as energy policy and the environment, third parties have long served as an important outlet for moving political debates forward. As a result, as we've repeatedly seen in American history, even when a third-party candidate loses, sometimes his ideas win.

Political scientist Daniel Mazmanian points out that "usually after a strong showing by a minor party, at least one of the major parties shifts its position, adopting the third party's rhetoric if not the core of its programs. Consequently, by the following election the third-party constituency . . . has a major party more sympathetic to its demands."*

This may be the least obvious, but possibly most important, element of a third-party run for the White House in 2008. We tend to think of elections as zero-sum games—and usually for good reason. But when it comes to a third-party candidate, a genuine opportunity exists for an independent to dictate the issues that come to the fore, not only on the campaign trail, but also after the election is over and governing begins.

ISSUES FOR 2008

If civil rights drove George Wallace and deficit spending and lobbying reform provided the impetus for Ross Perot, what potential issues could or should a third-party candidacy focus on in November? I believe that a number of issues are on the minds of the American people, who want more action and less talk.

*Quoted in Ronald Rapoport and Walter Stone, *Three's a Crowd* (Ann Arbor: University of Michigan Press, 2005).

The American people also want politicians to put all options on the table: increase taxes, cut entitlements, and, most of all, embrace shared sacrifice to enhance the common good. They recognize that our problems are too serious and our needs so substantial that every policy option *must* be on the table.

The American people have also become convinced that government in its current form is simply not working. We have not been able to defeat Al Qaeda, catch Osama bin Laden, or develop a comprehensive plan to fight terrorism or to extricate ourselves from Iraq—much less develop a comprehensive policy for the region. Domestic problems also appear to present a daunting challenge for which we have no answers. We have no clear plan to pay for our children's education, our own health care or retirement, or to provide for our aging parents. Further, we have natural disasters like Hurricane Katrina and man-made disasters such as the collapse of the bridge in Minneapolis for which we have no clear strategy for alleviating or preventing similar occurrences in the future. We are presented with partisan rhetoric and attack politics instead. And the American people are yearning for, even demanding, an end to the divisiveness and the development of policies that produce real results, not just sound bites.

What then are the specific issues for which we must have centrist, consensus-based policy prescriptions?

First and foremost, America needs a consensus on how to prosecute the war on terror—an issue that should and must rise above petty differences between the parties. At a time when America is facing the threat of international terrorism, we need a broad, national consensus on how to deal with America's enemies. There has been far too much focus on Iraq and not enough on the U.S. position in the Arab world and the kind of foreign and economic policies that will make America safer and less at risk from terrorism. Energy independence is crucial as well. The same goes for the burgeoning trade deficit, and the future of Social Security and other entitlement programs like Medicare and Medicaid.

Then there is immigration. This issue energizes millions of Americans. Many middle-class workers see illegal immigration as a threat to their jobs and their communities. They are concerned that illegal immigrants will take low-paying, menial jobs away from them by accepting lower salaries. Some social conservatives fear the corrosive effects of illegal immigration on the rule of law and detest the strain the immigrants have placed on border states' social-service budgets. Others appeal to xenophobia rather than economics. Millions of Hispanics and other immigrants see the issue as one of fairness. While we cannot leave our borders unprotected, we also cannot ignore the 12 million people who live in the country illegally. They must be able to work and gain a path to citizenship.

The failure of the immigration bill in the summer of 2007 provides an opening for a candidate in 2008 to focus on the issue with a proposal that keeps borders closed to new illegal immigrants but offers a route to citizenship for those who are already here. Such an approach would give a third-party candidate an advantage in the southwestern states as well as Florida, California, and Texas with their large immigrant populations. There is clearly a bipartisan solution to this problem—one that can win majority support with the American people—that a smart candidate can articulate in 2008.

Economic anxiety is, in my view, the underrated issue of the 2008 election. In the last several years, wage gains have remained small even as productivity has jumped. Between 2000 and 2005, productivity rose 17 percent, but the average take-home wage increased a meager 3 percent. In the five years before that, wages grew by 12 percent. In addition, family income is lower today than it was in 2000.*

*Krishna Guha, Edward Luce, and Andrew Ward, "Anxious Middle: Why Ordinary Americans Have Missed Out on the Benefits of Growth," *Financial Times*, November 2, 2006, p. 15.

This anemic wage growth and resulting insecurity creates political opportunities. But this doesn't mean Americans want massive new government programs. Focusing on the inequality between rich and poor may sound good for a partisan applause line, but it's a starting point for discussion, not a viable, long-term political solution. Americans want opportunity for all, rich and poor, not class warfare. They want expanded educational opportunities for their children—and themselves. That means retraining for workers dislocated by international trade and outsourcing as well as expanded student-loan programs.

In addition, with nearly 47 million Americans lacking health insurance and millions of others fearful of leaving their jobs and thus losing their health-care coverage, politicians need to make health care a top priority for 2008. An independent who focuses on a bipartisan program mixing government guarantees with a strong role for private insurance and a minimum of government bureaucracy would, in my view, garner strong support. Poll after poll demonstrates that Americans want lawmakers to tackle these challenges constructively and collegially. Yet Washington seems unable to do the people's business.

POLITICAL REFORM

Now that they control Congress, Democrats have begun to approach some of these pressing public policy issues. Clearly, however, more needs to be done. Indeed, the Congress could go a long way toward creating bipartisan solutions to these issues by bringing more transparency to government and tackling more directly the institutional corruption that so frequently delays policymaking in Washington.

If the 2006 election was in large measure a referendum on the Iraq War, it was also an indictment of corruption and ethics in government. When asked which issue was "extremely important," a higher number of voters cited corruption than any other issue, including the war.* More than three-fourths of voters said corruption influenced how they cast their ballot.†

True, the excesses of the GOP-led Congress, not to mention the Mark Foley congressional-page scandal, which broke only weeks before the election, accounted for these polling numbers. Democrats, however, would be foolish to believe that these issues have gone away. Almost a year after taking back the House and Senate, Democrats have yet to move forward with notable legislation on lobbying reform, campaign finance reform, or earmark reform. As Ross Perot did in 1992, an effective third-party candidate could certainly use foot-dragging on ending corruption in Washington as a key—and resonant—campaign theme.

In 2007, the House and Senate passed legislation that represented an important first step toward cleaning up Washington. The most important feature of this legislation was a measure forcing lobbyists to file reports on the "bundling" by one person or group of campaign contributions from many different sources. Bundling often provides lobbyists with far greater influence than if these contributions were provided individually. Such a measure would provide important transparency to the campaign finance system. Unfortunately, the bill remains trapped in a conference committee. With luck, by the time this book is published, it will be the law of the land.

The House passed a bill in July 2007 that banned lawmakers from paying their spouses for work performed on a campaign. The measure came after an outside study disclosed "that nearly 100 chairmen and ranking minority members of House committees

---

*"Corruption Named as Key Issue by Voters in Exit Polls," CNN, November 8, 2006, http://www.cnn.com/2006/POLITICS/11/07/election.exitpolls/index.html.
†"Exit Polls: Scandals Hurt GOP More Than War," Associated Press, November 7, 2006.

used their roles to benefit their families, including employing spouses and other kin for campaign or consulting work."* These measures, however, are only a first step. More must be done.

The Center on Congress at Indiana University has recommended, for example, that every detail of a member of Congress's encounter with a lobbyist should be publicly disclosed. This would help do away with the backroom meetings that too often have defined interactions between lobbyists and lawmakers. Moreover, lobbyists would have to disclose every dollar they spent to influence legislation, including not only campaign contributions, but also grassroots efforts and public relations campaigns. We're never going to keep lobbyists out of the halls of Congress, nor necessarily should we, but ensuring that their behavior is completely transparent would go a long way toward curbing excesses.†

Norman Ornstein of the American Enterprise Institute has taken lobbying reform a step further. He has called for the creation of an Office of Public Integrity that would be responsible for maintaining lobbyists' disclosure forms and would work to educate members and their staffs on proper rules for interacting with lobbyists. It would also establish a chief ethics officer for Congress.

This new ethics office would serve as an outside body, separate from Congress. While Congress would still make final judgments on ethics cases based on recommendations from this new entity, such an arrangement would help divorce the House and Senate from the often partisan nature of actual congressional ethics investigations. Ornstein urges the Congress to enact legislation that would ban members from soliciting contributions from any lob-

---

*Elizabeth Williamson, "House Passes Ban on Campaign Pay Going to Spouses," *Washington Post*, July 24, 2007.
†Lee Hamilton, "True Lobbying Reform," http://www.centeroncongress.org/radio_commentaries/true_lobbying_reform.php.

byist with business before the member and also close some loop-holes that permit lobbyists to entertain lawmakers.*

Thomas Mann of the Brookings Institution has also come forward with a number of reforms that deal not just with lobbying, but also congressional earmarks. For example, Mann has urged Congress to mandate that members list all their proposed earmarks in bills and elucidate the public policy purpose the earmarks purportedly serve. He also proposes that no earmarks be added to legislation after a conference committee had voted to approve the report.

Even my former colleague Dick Morris has come up with a number of proposals that I think merit some consideration:

- Banning all privately funded travel by Congress members.

- Requiring all members to document their travel and provide the information electronically for review by constituents.

- On earmarks, giving the president the power to impound specific appropriations—a power the office used to have, but no longer does.

The key point bringing all these proposed initiatives together is greater transparency in the legislative and campaign process. I believe that each of these efforts would go a long way toward proving the truth of the old expression "sunshine is the best disinfectant." From a political perspective, each of these initiatives would have the support of the American people and could form the backbone of a political platform on cleaning up corruption in Washington. Either Democrats or Republicans could move forward with these proposals, but an independent candidate unsullied by the ways of Washington would have a natural advantage.

---

*Testimony of Norman J. Ornstein, Resident Scholar, the American Enterprise Institute Hearing on "Lobbying Reform: Accountability through Transparency," Committee on Rules, U.S. House of Representatives, March 2, 2006, http://www.rules.house.gov/techouse/109/lobref/testimony/nornstein.pdf.

While these are important first steps, more could be done with fundamental reforms that go to the essence of our political system, reforms that would open up our democracy and provide greater citizen engagement and involvement. No one issue speaks more to the political system's corruption than campaign finance. Although the McCain-Feingold bill provided some important measures for cleaning up the system, it contained loopholes that were easily exploited by enterprising lobbyists and interest groups. How, then, can a political leader push forward an agenda of change in the financing of elections?

One idea that deserves greater scrutiny is the public financing of campaigns. Many countries around the world have taken this approach. Except for the sure-to-come barbs that such a policy represents "welfare for politicians," there's no good reason for it not to be considered.

One idea that goes beyond just the mechanisms of how campaigns are financed is to prevent incumbents with safe seats from funneling their money to contested districts or their party's leadership. Today, because gerrymandering creates so many safe congressional districts, many incumbents raise money they don't need—but which they can use on behalf of so-called party-building activities.

Creating more competitive districts and forcing more incumbents to work for their reelection would help to end this practice. In the short term, simply preventing incumbents from sharing their campaign largesse would help. Neither major party has the incentive to take such a step—but a third-party candidate could certainly raise awareness of the issue.*

*Steven Hill, "Lobbying Scandal Points to a Pyramid of Problems," *Atlanta Journal-Constitution*, April 27, 2006, http://www.newamerica.net/publications/articles/2006/lobbying_scandal_points_to_a_pyramid_of_problems.
†Ed Kilgore, "The Fix Is In," *Blueprint Magazine*, May 31, 2005.

CHANGES TO THE ELECTORAL SYSTEM

Beyond these incremental political changes, the most obvious place for potential reform is the nature of American elections. We're long overdue for a reexamination of the way we elect our presidents and how we choose our congressional leaders.

One area that must be addressed is the manner in which the so-called reapportionment committees gerrymander congressional districts. In order to protect incumbents from tough reelection battles, state legislatures make sure that only a fraction of congressional districts are at all competitive. According to a study by Gary Jacobson of the University of California at San Diego, 356 out of 435 congressional seats are considered safe, which leaves a scant 70 seats subject to competitive elections. Increasingly, legislators pick their voters rather than the proper other way around.[†]

Not only is this bad for the healthy exchange of ideas locally, but it also increases partisanship. When one party dominates a congressional district, it has a tendency to nominate and elect members from its extreme wing. Consequently, the need to reach across party lines and run to the middle practically doesn't exist in the majority of America's congressional districts.

Not only does this polarization contribute to the nation's toxic partisanship, it further turns off independent voters from even going to the polls. That's why the country should look more closely at a move being taken in Iowa to draw congressional districts in a nonpartisan manner. Iowa's nonpartisan redistricting maximizes competition within districts and often encourages centrist politicians to run for office in competitive elections. It's a long-overdue step and one that deserves greater consideration.

Another area desperately in need of reform is the Electoral College. Today, we have a system of electors in an arcane institution that is a winner-take-all proposition in all but two states.

That's why a candidate like Al Gore can win the popular vote and lose the election, as occurred in 2000. Of course, this isn't the first time that has happened. The popular-vote winner has lost the election three times in American history.

The main drawback of the Electoral College (besides its basic unfairness) is that it diminishes the votes of the people in states with small populations and only three, four, or five electoral votes. It causes the candidates to ignore those states during the campaign season. It's why only a very unwise Democratic presidential candidate would waste a minute in North Dakota. And it's also why candidates overwhelm the swing states with commercials and campaign stops, while states that are considered "solidly" red or blue barely rate an acknowledgment.

There are certainly better solutions than what we have now. Only two states have a progressive method of awarding their electoral votes: Maine and Nebraska. Instead of allotting all the votes to a plurality winner, these states divide their electoral votes along the lines of the popular vote. This system, if adopted more widely, would more equitably represent the voters' wishes. Such an approach would increase voter turnout and ensure greater involvement of all citizens in a state, not just the majority. It would create a far more representative democracy than we have now. It's the kind of reform that America needs more than ever.

Of course, such a method of choosing a president would greatly enhance the chances of a third-party candidate in several states. The best incentive for using this system is that intelligent people who like a third-party or independent candidate would no longer worry about "wasting" their vote for someone who couldn't win. (This was the main reason why droves of Nader supporters declined to vote for him in past elections.)

Opponents of such a method voice concerns that the presence of a third-party candidate could throw a vote into the House if no candidate receives an Electoral College majority. But if we used an "instant runoff" instead of plurality voting, such an outcome is less likely. In an instant runoff, voters list their candidates in order of preference. If a plurality isn't achieved on the first ballot, it eliminates the candidates with the fewest votes and recalibrates the results until there is a winner. Other countries have used this method and achieved satisfying results.

The most democratic possibility would be to institute direct presidential elections. Simply put, the person with the most votes would win the presidency, whether there were two or twenty candidates running. Another idea, floated by historian Arthur Schlesinger, would retain the Electoral College but give bonus electoral votes to the popular-vote winner, thus ensuring that even if the popular-vote winner lost the electoral vote, he or she could still become president.

I'm not holding my breath, of course, even if others agree that Schlesinger's idea is a sensible reform. It certainly would add zest to a race, however, to see a presidential hopeful showing up in Bismarck or Cheyenne or Provo or Eugene. Suddenly, it wouldn't be only the swing states that matter.

But above all, such an approach would encourage less partisanship. Voters in states that have for years been out of play could suddenly find themselves being sought after by the national campaigns. Democrats in Utah and Republicans in Massachusetts would matter a whole lot more. Candidates would have to consider these newly empowered voters. Such a change would, I believe, create more incentive to craft a broad-based message and would diminish the effectiveness of the narrow political messages we've seen in recent years.

CONCLUSION

All the measures I have outlined above achieve a singular and crucial goal: creating more transparency in government and forcing our nation's leaders to be more responsive to the will of the people. That is what Americans are demanding from Washington. Many like to argue that Americans hate their government, but the truth says otherwise. Americans want their elected leaders to tackle real problems in a bipartisan manner.

A recent Battleground Poll made clear the focus of the American people. By two to one, Americans prefer politicians who are committed to finding "practicable, workable solutions" versus ones who are defined by the strength of their "values and convictions."*

Americans see threats from abroad and diminished expectations at home. They believe their children's future will be less bright than their own. Above all, they are not interested in confrontation and polarization. They are far more focused on solutions. A third-party or independent candidate can drive that message home. He or she can run a campaign that focuses on ending corruption in Washington, crafting bipartisan solutions to the great challenges facing our nation, and strengthening the country's international position. An effective third-party candidacy can generate important debates on these questions—as third parties have done in America for nearly two centuries.

Of course, there is and always has been an alternative. The two parties can wake up to this reality and respond to it themselves. The choice and the solution are in their hands. What they decide will go a long way toward determining the nation's political future. The ball is in their court.

*Dan Balz, "Pessimism Nation," The Trail blog, WashingtonPost.com, July 27, 2007.

Acknowledgments

IN A CERTAIN SENSE, THIS WORK HAS BEEN THE PRODUCT OF MORE than thirty years of participation in and observation of the American political scene, and I owe a debt of gratitude to everyone who has taught me about practical politics and influenced my thinking. I want to specifically thank the people who made this book possible.

I would very much like to begin with Doug Garr, who did much of the early research on the book and was a source of many ideas and substantial input that aided the drafting of the manuscript. Michael Cohen also did research for the final section of the book and provided a number of compelling arguments about how the two parties have responded to the issue of bipartisanship. Carly Cooperman did a masterly job of providing both research and insights that have made this work immeasurably better than it otherwise would have been. My assistant, Jane Yoo, also played a central role in helping to organize my research as well as my life so that this book could be completed in a timely fashion. Scott Rasmussen provided an extraordinary amount of data happily and willingly, and a great deal of analysis as well. My friend and colleague David DesRosiers was also a great source of encouragement and advice.

I owe a substantial debt to Kurt Andersen, editor at large at Random House, himself both a supporter of centrist politics and a chronicler of third-party movements. Kurt was instrumental in both bringing the book to Random House and shaping its ultimate message. At Random House, I would very much like to thank Jonathan Jao for a superb job of editing in a very short time. Jonathan helped clarify my thinking and made the work immeasurably better. I also, of course, want to thank Gina Centrello, the president and publisher of Random House, who made a quick decision to publish the book and organized the team to accomplish that goal in such an efficient and professional manner.

In the end, this work is ultimately a direct result of those thirty years of active involvement in the American political scene. Despite the fact that I see much about the system that is operating far less efficiently than I would like, I remain optimistic about the ability of the system to ultimately meet the challenges facing America. At the very least, I hope this book will be a small contribution to ongoing efforts to create some degree of consensus and bipartisanship, and to address fundamental challenges we face as a nation.

Index

Page numbers in *italics* refer to figures and tables.

DOUGLAS E. SCHOEN was a campaign consultant for more than thirty years with the firm he founded, Penn, Schoen & Berland. He lives in New York City.

ABOUT THE TYPE

The text of this book was set in Filosofia. It was designed in 1996 by Zuzana Licko, who created it for digital typesetting as an interpretation of the sixteenth-century typeface Bodoni. Filosofia, an example of Licko's unusual font designs, has classical proportions with a strong vertical feeling, softened by rounded droplike serifs. She has designed many typefaces and is the cofounder of *Emigre* magazine, where many of them first appeared. Born in Bratislava, Czechoslovakia, Licko came to the United States in 1968. She studied graphic communications at the University of California at Berkeley, graduating in 1984.